THE PRESIDENTS

Editor

Fred L. Israel

VOLUME 6

Franklin D. Roosevelt 1933 – Lyndon B. Johnson 1969

Grolier Educational

SHERMAN TURNPIKE, DANBURY, CONNECTICUT

973
PRE

The publisher gratefully acknowledges permission from the sources to reproduce photos that appear on the cover.

Volume 1
J. Adams – New York Historical Society
J. Monroe – Library of Congress

Volume 2
J. K. Polk; A. Jackson; J. Tyler – Library of Congress
J. Q. Adams – National Archives

Volume 3
U. S. Grant – National Archives
A. Johnson; Z. Taylor – Library of Congress

Volume 4
B. Harrison; W. McKinley; J. A. Garfield – Library of Congress

Volume 5
H. Hoover; W. G. Harding – Library of Congress
T. Roosevelt – National Archives

Volume 6
D. D. Eisenhower – Library of Congress
L. B. Johnson – White House

Volume 7
B. Clinton – The White House
R. Reagan – Bush/Reagan Committee
G. Bush – Cynthia Johnson, The White House

Volume 8
T. Roosevelt – National Archives
B. Clinton – The White House

JH

Published 1997 exclusively for the school and library market by Grolier Educational

Sherman Turnpike, Danbury, Connecticut

© 1997 by Charles E. Smith Books, Inc.

Set: ISBN 0-7172-7642-2

Volume 6: ISBN 0-7172-7648-1

Library of Congress number:

The presidents.

p. cm.

Contents: v. 1. 1789–1825 (Washington–Monroe) — v. 2. 1825–1849 (Adams–Polk)

v. 3. 1849–1877 (Taylor–Grant) — v. 4. 1877–1901 (Hayes–McKinley) — v. 5.1901–1933 (T. Roosevelt–Hoover)

v. 6. 1933–1969 (F. D. Roosevelt–L. B. Johnson) — v. 7. 1969–1997 (Nixon–Clinton)

v. 8. Documents, suggested reading, charts, tables, appendixes

1. Presidents – United States – Juvenile literature.
[1. Presidents.]
E176.1.P9175   1997
973.099 — dc20

96-31491
CIP
AC

For information, address the publisher
Grolier Educational, Sherman Turnpike, Danbury, Connecticut 06816

Printed in the United States of America

Cover design by Smart Graphics

TABLE OF CONTENTS

VOLUME SIX

CONTRIBUTORS

EDITOR

Fred L. Israel received his Ph.D. from Columbia University. He has written several books for young adults including *Franklin D. Roosevelt, Henry Kissinger,* and *Know Your Government: The FBI.* Dr. Israel is also the editor of *History of American Presidential Elections, 1789–1968, The Chief Executive: Inaugural Addresses of the Presidents from George Washington to Lyndon Johnson,* and *The State of the Union Messages of the Presidents of the United States.* His most recent book is *Running for President, The Candidates and Their Images,* a two-volume work with Arthur M. Schlesinger, Jr. and David J. Frent.

Dr. Israel is Professor, Department of History, The City College of the City University of New York.

CONTRIBUTORS

Donald C. Bacon is a Washington-based journalist specializing in the presidency and Congress. He served as staff writer of *The Wall Street Journal* and assistant managing editor of *U.S. News and World Report.* A former Congressional Fellow, he is the author of *Rayburn: A Biography* and *Congress and You.* He is coeditor of *The Encyclopedia of the United States Congress.*

Hendrik Booraem V received his Ph.D. from The Johns Hopkins University. He taught social studies at Strom Thurmond High School, South Carolina, for many years. He has been Adjunct Professor at Rutgers University, Camden, Alvernia College, Lehigh University, and the State University of New York at Purchase. Dr. Booraem is the author of *The Formation of the Republican Party in New York: Politics and Conscience in the Antebellum North, The Road to Respectability: James A. Garfield and His World, 1844–1852,* and *The Provincial: Calvin Coolidge and His World, 1885–1895.*

Thomas Bracken received his B.A. and M.A., summa cum laude, from The City College of the City University of New York. He is currently enrolled in the doctoral program there, and he is Adjunct Professor of History.

David Burner received his Ph.D. from Columbia University. He is Professor of American History at the State University of New York at Stony Brook. Among Dr. Burner's many publications are *John F. Kennedy and a New Generation, The Torch is Passed: The Kennedy Brothers and American Liberalism* (with Thomas R. West) and *The Politics of Provincialism: The Democratic Party in Transition, 1918–1932.* He is also the coauthor of *Firsthand America: A History of the United States.*

Gary Cohn received his M.A. in Popular Culture Studies from Bowling Green State University in 1980 and has completed course work towards the doctorate in American History at the State University of New York at Stony Brook. As an Adjunct Professor he has taught history at The City College of the City University of New York and creative writing and composition at the C.W. Post campus of Long Island University.

Richard Nelson Current is University Distinguished Professor of History, Emeritus, at the University of North Carolina, Greensboro and former President of the Southern Historical Association. Among Dr. Current's many books are *Speaking of Abraham Lincoln: The Man and His Meaning for Our Times, Lincoln and the First Shot, The Lincoln Nobody Knows, Lincoln the President: Last Full Measure,* and with T. Harry Williams and Frank Freidel, *American History: A Survey.*

James B. Gardner received his Ph.D. from Vanderbilt University. He has been Deputy Executive Director of the American Historical Association since 1986 and Acting Executive Director of that organization since 1994. Dr. Gardner was with the American Association for State and Local History from 1979 to 1986, where he served in a variety of capacities, including Director of Education and Special Programs. Among his many publications is *A Historical Guide to the United States.*

Anne-Marie Grimaud received her B.A. from the Sorbonne, Paris and her M.A. from the State University of New York at Stony Brook, where she is currently enrolled in the doctoral program in American History.

Douglas Kinnard graduated from the United States Military Academy and served in Europe during World War II. He also served in Korea and Vietnam and retired as Brigadier General. He then received his Ph.D. from Princeton University. Dr. Kinnard is Professor Emeritus, University of Vermont and was Chief of Military History, U.S. Army. Among Dr. Kinnard's books are *Ike 1890–1990: A Pictorial History, President Eisenhower and Strategy Management: A Study in Defense Politics,* and *Maxwell Taylor and The American Experience in Vietnam.*

Robert A. Raber received his J.D. from the Law School, University of California, Berkeley. He retired from law practice and received his M.A. from The City College of the City University of New York, where he is enrolled in the doctoral program.

Donald A. Ritchie received his Ph.D. from the University of Maryland. Dr. Ritchie is on the Executive Committee of the American Historical Association, and he has been Associate Historian, United States Senate for 20 years. Among his many publications are *Press Gallery: Congress and the Washington Correspondents, The Young Oxford Companion to the Congress of the United States,* and *Oxford Profiles of American Journalists.*

Robert A. Rutland is Professor of History Emeritus, University of Virginia. He was editor in chief of *The Papers of James Madison* for many years, and he was coordinator of bicentennial programs at the Library of Congress from 1969 to 1971. Dr. Rutland is the author of many books including *Madison's Alternatives: The Jeffersonian Republicans and the Coming of War, 1805–1812, James Madison and the Search for Nationhood, James Madison: The Founding Father,* and *The Presidency of James Madison.* He is editor of *James Madison and the American Nation, 1751–1836: An Encyclopedia.*

Raymond W. Smock received his Ph.D. from the University of Maryland. He was involved with the Booker T. Washington Papers Project for many years and was coeditor from 1975 to 1983. He was Historian, Office of the Bicentennial, U.S. House of Representatives. In 1983, he was appointed as the first Director of the Office of the Historian of the U.S. House of Representatives. Among the major publications of that office are *The Biographical Directory of the United States Congress, 1774–1989, Black Americans in Congress, 1877–1989,* and *Women in Congress, 1917–1990.*

Darren D. Staloff received his Ph.D. from Columbia University, and he was a Post-Doctoral Fellow at the Institute of Early American History and Culture. He has taught at the College of Staten Island, Columbia University, and the College of William and Mary. Dr. Staloff is currently Assistant Professor of American History, The City College of the City University of New York. He is the author of *The Making of an American Thinking Class: Intellectuals and Intelligentsia in Puritan Massachusetts.*

John Stern received his M.A. from the State University of New York at Stony Brook, where he is enrolled in the doctoral program. His thesis is on Eugene McCarthy and the Presidential Campaign of 1968.

Edmund B. Sullivan received his Ed.D. from Fitchburg State College. He was Principal, New Hampton Community School, New Hampshire, and he taught at the North Adams and Newton public schools in Massachusetts. Dr. Sullivan was Professor at American International College and University of Hartford, and he was the founding Director and Curator of the Museum of American Political Life, West Hartford Connecticut. He is the author of *American Political Ribbons and Ribbon Badges, 1828–1988, American Political Badges and Medalets, 1789–1892,* and *Collecting Political Americana.*

Linda S. Vertrees received her B.A. in History from Western Illinois University and her M.A. in Library Science from the University of Chicago. She has written several annotated lists of suggested readings including the one for *The Holocaust, A Grolier Student Library.*

Thomas R. West received his Ph.D. from the Columbia University. He is Associate Professor, Department of History, Catholic University. He is coauthor, with David Burner, of *The Torch is Passed: The Kennedy Brothers and American Liberalism* and *Column Right: Conservative Journalists in the Service of Nationalism.*

INTRODUCTION

No branch of the federal government caused the authors of the Constitution as many problems as did the Executive. They feared a strong chief of state. After all, the American Revolution was, in part, a struggle against the King of England and the powerful royal governors. Surprisingly though, much power was granted to the president of the United States who is responsible only to the people. This was the boldest feature of the new Constitution. The president has varied duties. Above all, he must take care that the laws be faithfully executed. And also according to the Constitution, the president:

- is the commander in chief of the armed forces;
- has the power to make treaties with other nations (with the Senate's consent);
- appoints Supreme Court Justices and other members of the federal courts, ambassadors to other countries, department heads, and other high officials (all with the Senate's consent);
- signs into law or vetoes bills passed by Congress;
- calls special sessions of Congress in times of emergency.

In some countries, the power to lead is inherited. In others, men seize power through force. But in the United States, the people choose the nation's leader. The power of all the people to elect the president was not stated in the original Constitution. This came later. The United States is the first nation to have an elected president—and a president with a stated term of office. Every four years since the adoption of the Constitution in 1789, the nation has held a presidential election. Elections have been held even during major economic disruptions and wars. Indeed, these elections every four years are a vivid reminder of our democratic roots.

Who can vote for president of the United States? The original Constitution left voting qualifications to the states. At first, the states limited voting to white and very few black men who owned a certain amount of property. It was argued that only those with an economic or commercial interest in the nation should have a say in who could run the government. After the Civil War (1861–1865), the Fourteenth (1868) and Fifteenth (1870) Amendments to the Constitution guaranteed the vote to all men over the age of 21. The guarantee was only in theory. The Nineteenth Amendment (1920) extended the right to vote to women. The Nineteenth Amendment was a victory of the woman's suffrage movement which had worked for many years to achieve this goal. In 1964, the Twenty-fourth Amendment abolished poll taxes—a fee paid before a citizen was allowed to vote. This tax had kept many poor people, both black and white, from voting in several Southern states. And, the Twenty-sixth Amendment (1971) lowered the voting age to 18. (See Volume 8 for the complete text of the Constitution.)

In 1965, Congress passed the Voting Rights Act; it was renewed in 1985. This law, which carried out the requirements of the Fifteenth Amendment, made it illegal to interfere with anyone's right to vote. It forbade the use of literacy tests and, most important, the law mandated that federal voter registrars be sent into counties where less than 50 percent of the voting age population (black and white) was registered. This assumed that there must be serious barriers based on prejudice if so few had registered to vote. Those who had prevented African Americans from voting through fear and threat of violence now had to face the force of the federal government. Immediately, the number of African American voters in Southern states jumped dramatically from about 35 percent to 65 percent. In 1970, 1975, and 1982, Congress added amendments to the Voting Rights Act which helped other minorities such as Hispanics, Asians, Native Americans, and

Eskimos. For example, states must provide bilingual ballots in counties in which 5 percent or more of the population does not speak or read English. Today any citizen over the age of 18 has the right to vote in a presidential election. Many would argue that this is not only a right but also an obligation. However, all states deny the right to vote to anyone who is in prison.

Who can be president of the United States? There are formal constitutional requirements: one must be a "natural born citizen," at least 35 years old, and a resident of the United States for 14 years. The Constitution refers to the president as "he." It was probably beyond the thought process of the Founding Fathers that a woman, or a man who was not white, would ever be considered. The Twenty-second Amendment (1951), which deals with term limitations, uses "person" in referring to the president, recognizing that a woman could serve in that office.

How is the president elected? Most Americans assume that the president is elected by popular vote and the candidate with the highest number wins the election. This is not correct and may surprise those who thought they voted for Bill Clinton, Robert Dole, or Ross Perot in 1996. In fact, they voted for Clinton's or Dole's or Perot's electors who then elected the president. In the United States, the voters do not directly select the president. The Constitution provides a fairly complex—and some argue, an outdated—procedure for electing the president. Indeed, the electoral system devised by the Framers and modified by the Twelfth Amendment (1804) is unique. The records of the Constitutional Convention (1787) are silent in explaining the origins of the electoral system, usually referred to as the Electoral College. The several Federalist papers (Nos. 68–71) written by Alexander Hamilton in defense of the electoral system omit any source for the idea.

Under the electoral system of the United States, each state has the number of electoral voters equal to the size of its congressional delegation (House of Representatives plus Senate). Every 10 years, the census, as required by the Constitution, adjusts the number of representatives each state has in the House of Representatives because of population growth or loss. Every state always must have two senators. In the presidential election of 1996, for example, New York State had 33 electoral votes, because New York has 31 representatives and two senators. Alaska had three electoral votes, because Alaska has one representative and two senators. Since every congressional district must be approximately equal in population, we can say that the entire population of Alaska—the largest state in geographic size—is approximately equal in population to the 19th congressional district of New York City which covers the upper part of Manhattan Island.

There are 435 members of the House of Representatives. This number was fixed in 1910. There are 100 members of the Senate (50 states x 2 senators). This equals 535 electors. The Twenty-third Amendment (1961) gives the District of Columbia, the seat of our nation's capital, the electoral vote of the least populous state, three. So, the total electoral vote is 535 plus three or 538. To be elected president, a candidate must receive a majority, that is more than 50 percent, of the electoral votes: 270 electoral votes. If no candidate obtains a majority, the House of Representatives must choose the president from the top three candidates with each state delegation casting one vote. This happened in the 1824 presidential election. (See the article on John Quincy Adams.)

How does a political party choose its presidential nominee? Political parties play a crucial role—they select the candidates and provide the voters with a choice of alternatives.

In the early days of the Republic, the party's membership in Congress—the congressional caucus—chose presidential nominees. Sometimes state and local officials also put forward candidates. National party conventions where delegates were selected by state and local groups began by the 1830s. Each state had different delegate election procedures—some more democratic than others. Custom dictated that the convention sought the candidate. Potential nominees invariably seemed withdrawn and disinterested. They would rarely attend a nominating convention. Any attempt to pursue delegates was considered to be in bad taste. In fact, custom dictated that an official delegation went to the nominee's home to notify him of the party's decision and ask if he would accept. In the early years, convention officials sent a letter. By 1852, the candidate was informed in person. In the 1890s, these notification ceremonies dramatically increased in size. Madison Square Garden in New York City was the site for Grover Cleveland's 1892 notification.

By the first decade of the twentieth century, political reformers considered the convention system most undemocratic. They felt that it was a system dominated by patronage seeking party bosses who ignored the average voter. The primary system began as a way to increase participation in the nominating process. Candidates for the nation's highest office now actually sought the support of convention delegates. Theoretically, the primary allows all party members to choose their party's nominee. Most twentieth century conventions though, have seen a combination of delegates chosen by a political machine and elected in a primary. Today success in the primaries virtually assures the nomination. With few exceptions, the national conventions have become a rubber stamp for the candidate who did the best in the primaries.

The Campaign and Election. The presidential campaign is the great democratic exercise in politics. In recent elections, televised debates between the candidates have become a ritual, attracting record numbers of viewers. Public opinion polls continually monitor the nation's pulse. Commentators and writers analyze campaign strategies. Perhaps the winning strategy is to mobilize the party faithful and to persuade the independent voter that their candidate is the best. This is a costly process and since 1976, the general treasury provides major financial assistance to presidential campaigns. Public funding helps serious presidential candidates to present their qualifications without selling out to wealthy contributors and special interest groups.

Finally, on that first Tuesday after the first Monday in November, the voters make their choice. With the tragic exception of 1860, the American people have accepted the results. (See the article on Abraham Lincoln.) The election process works. Democracy has survived. Forty-one men have held the office of president of the United States. Each has been a powerful personality with varied leadership traits. Each had the opportunity to make major decisions both in foreign and domestic matters which affected the direction of the nation.

Join us as we proceed to study the men who helped to shape our history. We will also learn about their vice presidents, their cabinets, their families, and their homes and monuments.

Fred L. Israel
The City College of the City University of New York

ACKNOWLEDGMENTS

Sir Isaac Newton, the seventeenth-century English scientist who created calculus, discovered that white light is composed of many colors, discovered the law of gravity, and developed the standard laws of motion, once said, "If I have seen farther, it is because I have stood on the shoulders of giants." He meant that he used the work of those who came before him as a starting point for the development of his own ideas. This concept is as true in reference books as it is in science.

The White House Historical Association (740 Jackson Place N.W., Washington, D.C. 20503) supplied all the full page color paintings of the presidents, except seven. They are used with the permission of the White House

Historical Association, and we are grateful to them for their cooperation. The painting of James Monroe is Courtesy of the James Monroe Museum and Memorial Library, Fredericksburg, Virginia; the William Henry Harrison portrait is Courtesy of Grouseland; the John Tyler painting is Courtesy of Sherwood Forest Plantation; the Benjamin Harrison painting is from the President Benjamin Harrison Home; Harry Truman's photograph is from the U.S. Navy, Courtesy Harry S. Truman Library; George Bush's photograph is Courtesy of the Bush Presidential Materials Project; Bill Clinton's photograph is Courtesy of The White House. All the busts of the vice presidents are Courtesy of the Architect of the Capitol.

Over three dozen illustrations are credited to the Collection of David J. and Janice L. Frent. The Frents are friends and neighbors. Fred Israel and I both want to thank them very much for allowing us to show some of the treasures of their unequaled collection of political memorabilia.

The authors of the biographical pieces on the presidents are listed in each volume. They have provided the core of this work, and I am very grateful to them for their cooperation. Dr. Donald A. Ritchie, Associate Historian, United States Senate, wrote all the biographies of the vice presidents. Few people know more about this subject than Dr. Ritchie, and we appreciate his assistance.

Maribeth A. Corona (Editor, Charles E. Smith Books, Inc.) and I have written the sections on Family, Cabinet, and Places. Dr. Israel's editing of our work corrected and improved it greatly although we take full responsibility for any errors that remain. In preparing the material on places, three books served as a starting point: *Presidential Libraries and Museums, An Illustrated Guide,* Pat Hyland (Congressional Quarterly Inc., 1995); *Historic Homes of the American Presidents,* second edition, Irvin Haas (Dover Publications, 1991); and *Cabins, Cottages & Mansions, Homes of the Presidents of the United States,* Nancy D. Myers Benbow and Christopher H. Benbow (Thomas Publications, 1993). We wrote to every place noted in this work and our copy is based on the wealth of information returned to us. It is the most comprehensive and up-to-date collection of information available on this subject.

There is no single book on the families of the presidents. We relied on the abundance of biographies and autobiographies of members of the first families. Also helpful was *Children in the White House,* Christine Sadler (G.P. Putnam's Sons, 1967); *The Presidents' Mothers,* Doris Faber (St. Martin's Press, 1978); and *The First Ladies,* Margaret Brown Klapthor (White House Historical Association, 1989).

The Complete Book of U.S. Presidents, William A. DeGregorio (Wings Books, 1993) is an outstanding one-volume reference work, and we referred to it often. I also had the great pleasure of referring often to three encyclopedias which I had published earlier: *Encyclopedia of the American Presidency,* Leonard W. Levy and Louis Fisher (Simon & Schuster, 1994); *Encyclopedia of the American Constitution,* Leonard W. Levy, Kenneth L. Karst, and Dennis Mahoney (Macmillan & Free Press, 1986); and *Encyclopedia of the United States Congress,* Donald C. Bacon, Roger Davidson, and Morton H. Keller (Simon & Schuster, 1995). I also referred often to *Running for President, The Candidates and Their Images,* Arthur M. Schlesinger, Jr. (Simon & Schuster, 1994). Publishing this two-volume set also gave me the pleasure of working with Professor Schlesinger and the Associate Editors, Fred L. Israel and David J. Frent.

Most of the copyediting was done by Jerilyn Famighetti who was, as usual, prompt, accurate, and pleasant. Our partner in this endeavor was M.E. Aslett Corporation, 95 Campus Plaza, Edison, New Jersey. Although everyone at Aslett lent a hand, special thanks go to Elizabeth Geary, who designed the books; Brian Hewitt and Bob Bovasso, who scanned the images; and Joanne Morbit, who composed the pages. They designed every page and prepared the film for printing. The index was prepared by Jacqueline Flamm.

Charles E. Smith
Freehold, New Jersey

Franklin D. Roosevelt

32ND PRESIDENT
OF THE UNITED STATES OF AMERICA

CHRONOLOGICAL EVENTS

30 January 1882	Born, Hyde Park, New York
24 June 1903	Graduated from Harvard University, Cambridge, Massachusetts
8 November 1910	Elected to New York State Senate
1913	Appointed assistant secretary of the navy
2 November 1920	Defeated for election as vice president
1921	Stricken by polio (poliomyelitis) at Campobello Island, New Brunswick
6 November 1928	Elected governor of New York
4 November 1930	Reelected governor of New York
8 November 1932	Elected president
4 March 1933	Inaugurated president
9 March 1933	Signed Emergency Banking Act
12 March 1933	First "fireside chat"
31 March 1933	Signed Civilian Conservation Corps Reconstruction Act
13 May 1933	Signed Agricultural Adjustment Act
18 May 1933	Signed Tennessee Valley Authority Act
16 June 1933	Signed National Industrial Recovery Act
5 July 1935	Signed National Labor Relations Act (Wagner-Connery Act)
14 August 1935	Signed Social Security Act
3 November 1936	Reelected president
20 January 1937	Inaugurated president
5 November 1940	Reelected president
20 January 1941	Inaugurated president
11 March 1941	Signed Lend-Lease Act
14 August 1941	Announced Atlantic Charter
7 December 1941	Pearl Harbor, Hawaii attacked by Japanese air and naval forces
8 December 1941	Signed declaration of war against Japan
24 January 1943	Met with Prime Minister Winston Churchill, Casablanca, Morocco
28 November 1943	Met with Prime Minister Churchill and Marshal Joseph Stalin, Teheran, Iran
7 November 1944	Reelected president
20 January 1945	Inaugurated president
3–7 February 1945	Met with Prime Minister Churchill and Marshal Stalin, Yalta, U.S.S.R
12 April 1945	Died, Warm Springs, Georgia

BIOGRAPHY

Franklin Delano Roosevelt became the thirty-second president of the United States in 1933, amid the nation's worst economic depression. In an effort to improve the economy, his administration greatly increased the powers of government. During World War II, he led the United States military to victory as the commander in chief, and he was instrumental in setting up the United Nations in order to create a lasting peace. History regards Roosevelt as one of the strongest and most popular chief executives.

EARLY YEARS. Franklin D. Roosevelt was born on 30 January 1882 at his family's estate in Hyde Park, New York, located on a cliff high above the Hudson River, a few miles north of Poughkeepsie. His father, James, was of Dutch ancestry. A wealthy railroad executive, he had been married once before. Franklin's mother, Sara Delano, a descendant of French Huguenots, was 27 years younger than her husband. Franklin was the only child of this marriage. His father traveled in elite circles, dined at the White House, and counted President Grover Cleveland among his friends. James Roosevelt remained a lifelong Democrat in a family and a circle of Republicans.

As a boy, Roosevelt learned lessons of social responsibility from his father and his French governess. At the age of 11, he became an avid stamp collector. This hobby, along with several trips to Europe, afforded Roosevelt the opportunity to learn much about geography, foreign affairs, and world history. Like his cousin Theodore, Franklin developed a keen interest in ornithology (the branch of zoology that concerns itself with the study of birds). He collected more than 300 species of birds. His most beloved hobby, however, was sailing. He first sailed with his father at the family's vacation home at Campobello, a small Canadian island in the Bay of Fundy. He returned there often throughout his life.

When he turned 14, Roosevelt entered the Groton Episcopal Church school, an exclusive preparatory school in Groton, Massachusetts. Living conditions at Groton were harsher and more disciplined than those he enjoyed at Hyde Park, but Roosevelt enjoyed his education immensely. He did well at history, algebra, and classic literature, which made up his basic studies. He was less successful at sports. At Groton his commitment to public service took root. The success of his cousin, Theodore Roosevelt, then assistant secretary of the navy, increased his interest in politics. Franklin wrote an essay at Groton on the moral perils of U.S. imperialism, specifically, the annexation of Hawaii.

After four years at Groton, Roosevelt entered Harvard University, where he received a liberal arts education. Roosevelt never distinguished himself as a student in college. After being rejected by the prestigious Porcellian Club (a club that had accepted his cousin Theodore, who was the president of the United States by then), he turned his attention to the Harvard *Crimson*, the student newspaper. He started as an editor and eventually became president of the paper. In 1900, his father died, and his mother, always central to his life, now grew more domineering.

Roosevelt had first met his distant cousin Eleanor when he was four, and she, two. Now at age 20 he often saw his cousin at dances, and his attraction to her grew into love. Against his mother's wishes, Franklin and Eleanor married in New York City on St. Patrick's Day, 1905. President Theodore Roosevelt gave away the bride, his niece. The Roosevelts would have six children; one died in infancy. The family lived at the estate at Hyde Park, and at a home in New York City, and vacationed at Campobello.

EARLY POLITICAL CAREER. Roosevelt attended Columbia University Law School after Harvard and passed the bar in 1907. He then became an unsalaried law clerk with a leading New York law firm. Although he possessed an average legal mind, his attractive looks, winning personality, and family connections soon brought him a partnership, but the legal profession bored him. Politics, however, lit a fire in Roosevelt, and his outgoing personality made him an obvious choice for public office. In 1910, the Democratic organization of Dutchess County nominated him for the New York State Senate. He was well liked among local leaders, and the Roosevelt name assured financial support for the party. But the Tammany Hall Democratic political machine of New York City feared his candidacy because of the independence that his wealth provided. Moreover, the district in which he was running, the twenty-sixth, was solidly Republican. Roosevelt therefore faced a struggle. He became one of the first candidates in the country to run his campaign from an automobile. While touring the district and making hundreds of speeches, he displayed a pleasant and likable disposition, although his inexperience often showed. On the campaign trail, he attacked political bosses and corruption, and first used his trademark phrase, "my fellow Americans." Roosevelt was elected by a narrow margin on the wave of a statewide Democratic victory and a national trend toward progressive politics.

Within six months of taking office in January 1911, Roosevelt led a group that revolted against Tammany Hall and defeated its candidate for the U.S. Senate, William F. Sheehan. He supported direct popular election of senators, the Seventeenth Amendment, which was ratified in 1913. He also publicly supported woman's suffrage as early as 1912. Roosevelt had no part, however, in progressive labor legislation for fear of angering his considerable agricultural support in the district. He worked vigorously for cheaper power rates that would help farmers and against Tammany-sponsored bills that would benefit special interest groups. In 1912, he was overwhelmingly reelected, and was promptly appointed chairman of the Senate Committee on Agriculture. He used his post to push through the legislature a series of agricultural bills, including one that ended the unfair commissions charged to farmers by merchants.

Roosevelt led the New York delegation to the Democratic convention at Baltimore in 1912. His choice for the nominee was New Jersey Governor Woodrow Wilson. When Wilson became president, he did not forget Roosevelt's strong support and offered him several positions in his administration. Roosevelt chose the one that his cousin Theodore had held on his path to the presidency, assistant secretary of the navy. During Roosevelt's eight-year tenure as assistant to Secretary of the Navy Josephus Daniels, he introduced administrative changes to improve the efficiency of the department. A devoted admirer of Captain Alfred Thayer Mahan, who had preached naval supremacy as the key to world leadership, Roosevelt favored the expansion and readiness of the navy. He frequently took an aggressive stance in diplomatic debates over the appropriate U.S. role in events such as the Mexican civil war. He often clashed with Secretary Daniels and even President Wilson, but remained a popular and attractive figure. In 1914, Roosevelt suffered his first political defeat in a primary race for U.S. senator from New York.

When war broke out in Europe, Roosevelt, considered more of a naval expert than his superior, took virtual control of the Navy Department. Again

James M. Cox (left), three-term governor of Ohio, chose Assistant Secretary of the Navy Franklin D. Roosevelt as his vice presidential running mate in 1920. They lost to Warren G. Harding and Calvin Coolidge. (Courtesy Library of Congress.)

3

he supported increasing the military's capabilities to protect U.S. interests. However, President Wilson was reelected in 1916 on a platform of non-intervention. Congress was inclined to agree with his pacifist sentiments. After U.S. entry into the war, Roosevelt's contribution was more noticeable.

Roosevelt resigned his post as assistant secretary in 1920 to accept the nomination for vice president to run with James M. Cox of Ohio, the presidential nominee. They backed Wilson's League of Nations and supported many other progressive Wilsonian positions. But the voters were tired of Democratic policies, and cautious of further foreign entanglements. As Wilson lay partially paralyzed from a stroke, the country gave a resounding victory to Warren G. Harding. Roosevelt then returned to the law partnership that he had formed earlier in 1920.

BATTLE WITH POLIO. Nineteen twenty-one brought a sudden and seemingly irreversible change of fortune to Roosevelt's rise to the top. In August he was struck by infantile paralysis, or polio, after swimming near Campobello Island. After months of illness in which he came close to dying, he began a remarkable comeback. He would never regain the use of his legs. Heavy steel braces and a cane or crutches would guide his walk, often with the help of someone's arm. His spirit, though, remained unbroken, and he was committed to gaining his place in history.

His physical disability also brought a change in his wife, Eleanor. For the first time she became actively interested in his political career. She would serve as his legs and go to the places and speak to the people that he could not. She grew more assertive and became involved in women's issues. At this time Roosevelt discovered Warm Springs, Georgia, a place whose "curative" waters would help his rehabilitation. The exercises he did in the spring water that filled the resort's pool strengthened his upper torso and even helped his withered legs achieve their fullest capacity. Ultimately, he established a treatment center there in order to help other victims of paralysis.

Roosevelt founded the law firm of Roosevelt and O'Connor in 1924. He threw his political weight behind New York's Roman Catholic Governor Alfred E. Smith in the presidential election of that year. He became his campaign manager and delivered his nominating speech. He made a national name for himself with his rousing speech, calling Smith the "happy warrior." His appearance was made all the more moving when the delegates saw him struggle courageously to the podium on crutches. Smith lost the nomination when a deadlocked convention turned to John W. Davis, a wealthy corporate lawyer, as their compromise candidate. Another Republican landslide occurred in 1924, and Calvin Coolidge was elected president.

GOVERNOR. President Calvin Coolidge decided against running for reelection in 1928, and the Republican nomination went to Secretary of Commerce Herbert Hoover. Governor Alfred E. Smith was chosen again as the Democratic candidate after four terms as governor of New York. Smith knew that he would have to carry his home state to have any realistic chance of winning the election. He needed someone of Roosevelt's stature to run for governor to accomplish this. Initially reluctant, Roosevelt finally agreed to run under pressure from the party regulars whose support he would need in the not-too-distant future. Roosevelt had planned to run for the governorship in 1932 and for the presidency in 1936. Roosevelt stressed state issues such as agriculture and labor in the campaign and won the governorship in the face of yet another Republican presidential landslide. With his victory, Roosevelt became the favorite to capture the Democratic presidential nomination in 1932.

As governor, Roosevelt exercised progressive leadership. He battled the utilities that tried to seize St. Lawrence River hydroelectric power to increase their already sizable profits. He also developed legislation to give relief to poor farmers, and supported old-age pensions, and unemployment insurance. He convinced the state legislature to pass a law limiting the working hours of women and children.

After his reelection as governor by a wide margin in 1930, Roosevelt appointed a commission to clean up Tammany Hall corruption. He moved cautiously against Tammany, because he would need the help of other big city machines if he was to be successful in a presidential bid. Yet the Republicans, and some in his own party, would be sure to attack any reluctance on his part to dismantle Tammany.

For years, Roosevelt had seen the coming of a strong national economic downturn. But he, as well as other Americans, was unprepared for what was to come after the stock market crash of 1929.

ELECTION OF 1932. Roosevelt saw the seeds of the depression as emerging from the enduring agricultural recession, so he campaigned for the 1932 Democratic nomination for president with a pledge to raise the purchasing power of the farmer. He also promised to help the middle classes who were losing their homes to mortgage foreclosures. From the beginning of his campaign, Roosevelt captured the imagination of many Americans. However, the nomination went to Roosevelt only after his campaign manager, James A. Farley, made a deal with House Speaker John Nance Garner. To encourage him to release his delegates, Garner was offered—and accepted—the vice presidential spot.

The campaign of 1932 drew sharp contrasts between the candidates. When thousands of World War I veterans camped in Washington to pressure Congress into paying them their bonuses scheduled for distribution at a later date, President Hoover ordered the army to remove them from the district. For his part, Roosevelt pledged a "New Deal" for the United States including federal relief, refinancing of home and farm mortgages, a lower tariff, repeal of prohibition, a voluntary crop control program, reforestation, regulation of securities sales, self-sustaining public works, and economy in government. Roosevelt defeated President Hoover by an overwhelming margin, and a new era had begun.

PRESIDENT. The depression destroyed the nation's economy. Within the first three years national income was cut in half; about 12 million men and women joined the ranks of the unemployed; bank failures wiped out life savings; thousands of factories shut down; many mines were closed; and railroads went bankrupt. By March 1933, more than 20 states had declared bank "holidays" to stop panic withdrawals. Governor Herbert Lehman closed all banks and stock exchanges in New York. A few days later, banking operations halted nationwide. The economic life of the country came to a virtual standstill.

THE NEW DEAL. In his Inaugural Address on 4 March 1933, Roosevelt promised to use "direct vigorous action," be it by rapid legislative change or broad executive emergency powers as in wartime. If forced, Roosevelt would become the benevolent dictator, a role he had seen President Wilson play during World War I. Roosevelt, in fact, built a broad alliance in Congress in order to push through his legislation more easily. He would try a plan; if it failed, he would try something else. To deal with the crisis he was aided by advisers such as Rexford Tugwell, who would become assistant secretary of agriculture; Raymond Moley, assistant secretary of state; Henry Wallace, secretary of agriculture; Harry Hopkins, special assistant; and Harold Ickes, secretary of the interior, among others. The first business of the New Deal was to restore the purchasing power of farmers and to stimulate industrial recovery. Legislation would target banking, industry and labor, hydroelectric power, and many other parts of American life.

Roosevelt's first actions upon taking office were borrowed from his predecessors. He declared a national banking holiday, preventing a further run on banks. He then submitted to Congress an emergency banking bill that had been drafted under President Hoover. It permitted sound banks to reopen and authorized the issue of Federal Reserve notes to meet future bank failures. For the long term, the banks could issue preferred stock. On the basis of this security, the Reconstruction Finance Corporation (RFC) could lend funds to

First Inaugural Address

. . . This is pre-eminently the time to speak the truth, the whole truth, frankly and boldly. Nor need we shrink from honestly facing conditions in our country today. This great nation will endure as it has endured, will revive and will prosper.

So first of all let me assert my firm belief that the only thing we have to fear is fear itself—nameless, unreasoning, unjustified terror which paralyzes needed efforts to convert retreat into advance.

In every dark hour of our national life a leadership of frankness and vigor has met with that understanding and support of the people themselves which is essential to victory. I am convinced that you will again give that support to leadership in these critical days.

In such a spirit on my part and on yours we face our common difficulties. They concern, thank God, only material things. Values have shrunken to fantastic levels; taxes have risen; our ability to pay has fallen, government of all kinds is faced by serious curtailment of income; the means of exchange are frozen in the currents of trade; the withered leaves of industrial enterprise lie on every side; farmers find no markets for their produce; the savings of many years in thousands of families are gone.

More important, a host of unemployed citizens face the grim problem of existence, and an equally great number toil with little return. Only a foolish optimist can deny the dark realities of the moment. Yet our distress comes from no failure of substance. We are stricken by no plague of locusts. Compared with the perils which our forefathers conquered because they believed and were not afraid, we have still much to be thankful for. Nature still offers her bounty and human efforts have multiplied it. Plenty is at our doorstep, but a generous use of it languishes in the very sight of the supply.

Primarily, this is because the rulers of the exchange of mankind's goods have failed through their own stubbornness and their own incompetence, have admitted their failure and abdicated. Practices of the unscrupulous money changers stand indicted in the court of public opinion, rejected by the hearts and minds of men. . . .

Recognition of the falsity of material wealth as the standard of success goes hand in hand with the abandonment of the false belief that public office and high political position are to be valued only by the standards of pride of place and personal profit; and there must be an end to a conduct in banking and in business which too often has given to a sacred trust the likeness of callous and selfish wrongdoing.

Small wonder that confidence languishes, for it thrives only on honesty, on honor, on the sacredness of obligations, on faithful protection, on unselfish performance. Without them it cannot live.

Restoration calls, however, not for changes in ethics alone. This nation asks for action, and action now.

Our greatest primary task is to put people to work. This is no unsolvable problem if we face it wisely and courageously. . . .

It can be accomplished in part by direct recruiting by the government itself, treating the task as we would treat the emergency of a war, but at the same time, through this employment, accomplishing greatly needed projects to stimulate and reorganize the use of our natural resources. . . .

• *President Roosevelt delivered his first Inaugural Address on 4 March 1933. He announced his plans for a "New Deal" and stirred the country with his memorable words: "The only thing we have to fear is fear itself."*

keep the banks open. The federal insurance of deposits came soon after although Roosevelt initially opposed it. It is generally considered one of the most notable achievements of the Roosevelt administration.

The first bill to pass Congress was the key to the nation's recovery in the President's estimation. This legislation created the controversial Agricultural Adjustment Administration (AAA), designed to cut crop surpluses by paying farmers to accept government controls. The bill had to be passed quickly, according to the President, lest "the effect on the prices of this year's crops be wholly lost." Conservatives thought that the AAA bordered on socialism, but that did not stop Roosevelt. The bill called for farmers growing corn, wheat, cotton, and other staples for foreign trade to place their operations under the control of the secretary of agriculture. He would reduce overproduction by shifting part of the land to soil-improving crops. Subsidies would be paid to the farmers for their cooperation. The law would control most of the 6 million U.S. farms, although participation was entirely voluntary. As part of the plan, the President could inflate the currency by reducing the gold content of the dollar. The cheaper money, it was believed, would raise crop prices. The bill also provided for federal loans to farmers at low interest rates. Secretary of Agriculture Wallace succeeded in taking nearly 66 million acres out of production in 1934–1935, and the income of farmers rose by a third. Most farmers liked the plan, but critics claimed that most of the benefits went to large farms. In addition, they argued that it was immoral to withhold food when people were hungry.

Next, Roosevelt pushed his economy program through Congress. This plan, in effect, cut government salaries and veterans' pensions to reduce the federal budget. The number of government personnel was also reduced, as was the defense budget, by one third, for fiscal 1934.

In 1933 the World Economic Conference, devised to minimize trade barriers and stabilize world currencies, took place in London. Roosevelt appointed Secretary of State Cordell Hull to be head of the United States delegation. The President believed that the dollar had not dropped to its proper level and that this would threaten his domestic program for raising prices. Roosevelt had already taken the United States off the gold standard, allowing the dollar to drop from its artificially high level. He disappointed the other delegations by rejecting their stabilization program, and the conference ended in failure. To Roosevelt, the value of the dollar was more important than an international agreement. Many, at home and abroad, thought that the President had passed up a good opportunity to deal with the world depression.

Roosevelt set up the Civilian Conservation Corps (CCC), to relieve unemployment among the young at home. The CCC provided meals, uniforms, housing, and a small fee to 250,000 young men for work on government projects such as replanting forests. The Public Works Administration (PWA) gave people work constructing roads, dams, and public buildings. Yet another bill created the Federal Emergency Relief Administration (FERA), which made grants to states for relief projects. Equally important in lessening the financial pressures was putting an end to the fraud and misrepresentation in stock and bond sales that had robbed millions of their savings. The Securities Act, requiring full financial disclosure was passed, to be followed by the establishment of the Securities and Exchange Commission (SEC). To lessen the economic burden on the railroads, the Emergency Railroad Transportation Act provided reorganization and coordination. When economic conditions improved slightly, railroad executives lost interest and Congress watered down the legislation.

The National Industrial Recovery Act of 1933 was supposed to be the interacting agency of three interest groups—business, labor, and consumers—and was considered by many more radical in concept than the Agricultural Adjustment Administration. For business, it would end cutthroat competition by having the federal government support trade association codes of fair practice. Labor would obtain benefits such as minimum wage guarantees, and consumer interests would be protected. To administer this law, the National Recovery Administration (NRA) was formed under the leadership of General Hugh S. Johnson. Roosevelt's critics regarded this bill as an abandonment of trust-busting, for it was hard to distinguish the price-fixing practices of trade associations from those of monopolies. Under General Johnson's direction, the NRA drafted 557 basic codes, of which 441 fixed prices. The codes banned child labor, raised wages, reduced working hours, and tried to create more jobs, but the law quickly grew unpopular since it seemed to make goods more expensive. Small businesses were hurt because their costs were higher than those of big businesses. Moreover, the codes were considered overly complicated, requiring experts to explain them. Still another complaint of labor was that big businesses evaded collective bargaining by forming company unions. The government tried to mediate these grievances by setting up a review board, presided over by the lawyer Clarence Darrow.

Ultimately the Supreme Court ruled the NRA unconstitutional on the grounds that the law used to create this legislation conferred on the executive branch powers to regulate the economy that under the Constitution could belong only to Congress.

The NRA generated a great expansion of organized labor. The National Labor Relations Act, (also known as the Wagner-Connery Act) was passed in 1935 guaranteeing the right of bargain collectively. The American Federation of Labor (AFL), headed by William Green, had fewer than 2.5 million craft members in 1933. A new organization led by John L. Lewis, the Congress of Industrial Organizations (CIO), was created in the 1930s to organize semiskilled workers. Union membership grew to 12 million by 1943.

One of Roosevelt's most innovative reforms that he long fought for was cheap hydroelectric power. During World War I, a huge dam was built at Muscle Shoals on the Tennessee River in order to provide electric power for nitrate plants. A fight developed over whether public or private interests would control the Tennessee River's water power in the postwar era. President Hoover favored private ownership, while the progressive Nebraska Senator George W. Norris lobbied for public control of hydroelectric plants. Roosevelt created the Tennessee Valley Authority (TVA) in 1933 to develop all of the water and power sources of the Tennessee River and to promote the economic and social well-being of the Tennessee Valley by providing cheap electric power.

By 1935, the effects of the depression had lessened slightly, but unemployment and poverty were still widespread. The President now called for a more just and fairer redistribution of wealth. Declaring that each citizen must be guaranteed "a proper security, a reasonable leisure, and a decent living throughout life," he proposed social security measures based on the British model for providing insurance for unemployment and old age. The Social Security Act was passed in 1935. Under it the unemployed and the aged would be guaranteed security by a combination of state and federal government. An unemployment insurance fund would be paid for by a national tax withheld from payrolls, while the federal government would help the states pay pensions to the elderly by creating a separate annuity system based on a wage-earner's and employer's contributions. This would guarantee every contributor a modest pension at age 65.

Other notable accomplishments of the first New Deal included the National Youth Administration (NYA), created to provide part-time jobs for high-school and college students and part-time employment for out-of-school youth, and the Rural Electrification Administration (REA), developed to bring electricity to rural areas. An important part of the recovery effort was the Works Progress Administration (WPA) created by the Emergency Relief Appropriation Act, passed in 1935.

The President in 1935 extended his alliance with workers and a large portion of the public with the Banking Act, allowing more federal control of the nation's banking system, and the Wealth Tax Act. These two laws drew sharp attacks on Roosevelt from Republicans who believed he was building a group opposed to business and the well-to-do. Yet Roosevelt still intended mainly to strengthen and prolong the capitalist system and its free-market economy.

ELECTION OF 1936. Roosevelt's new reforms, termed the Second New Deal, were intended to reelect him in 1936. But after almost four years of Roosevelt's administration, unemployment continued to be seriously high. On 27 June 1936, the President used the new communications medium of radio to rally public opinion for still further social and economic legislation. In one of his fireside chats, begun in 1933, he said, "There is a mysterious cycle to human events. To some generations much is given. Of others much is expected. This generation of Americans has a rendezvous with destiny." Roosevelt also had to face attacks from rabble-rousers such as Detroit's Father Charles Coughlin, a right-wing Roman Catholic priest; California's Francis E. Townsend, the originator of a plan for helping the elderly; and William Dudley Pelly of the far-right Silver Shirts. All were anti-Roosevelt, but none supported the Republican Party.

On election night 1936, Roosevelt, with 60 percent of the popular vote, easily outpolled his Republican opponent, Governor Alfred E. Landon of Kansas. Landon, while campaigning for unemployment relief, farm subsidies, collective bargaining, and antitrust action, had denounced the New Deal as socialist and unconstitutional. Roosevelt owed his landslide reelection to an alliance of farmers, labor unions, and city political machines. This alliance defined the Democratic Party and would continue to dominate national politics, especially Congress, for decades.

The Supreme Court set back the reform movement in two notable cases. In *United States v. Butler* (1936), the justices ruled the Agricultural Adjustment Administration unconstitutional. The Court ruled that in creating it Congress had overstepped its taxing power. Then, in *Morehead v. New York ex. rel. Tipaldo* (1936), the Court overturned a New York State law giving women a minimum wage. Roosevelt grew impatient waiting for a liberal majority on the Court. Early in 1937, he revealed a plan to add 35 district judges to speed the judicial process and to appoint six Supreme Court justices for those justices who were past 70 years of age and did not retire. Republicans and conservative Democrats denounced this court-packing scheme as ending the checks and balances system within the federal government and establishing a dictatorship of the executive. Roosevelt was unable to get the legislation passed, but the Court shifted its decisions in his favor. Between 1937 and 1945 he was to appoint eight new, liberal justices. He also appointed Harlan Fiske Stone chief justice in 1941. Stone had been on the Court since 1925.

During the winter of 1937–1938, the Depression worsened when federal relief programs were cut in favor of a balanced budget. Influenced by the deficit-spending theories of economist John Maynard Keynes, Roosevelt proposed $3 billion in public works that Congress rapidly passed. The sum, however, was too small to restart the economy. Other legislation was tried: a second AAA to limit agricultural overproduction; the Fair Labor Standards Act of 1938 to set a minimum wage; and the Wagner-Steagall National Housing Act to increase the availability of homes for middle-class families.

The New Deal was not able to end the Depression, but its relief measures helped millions of Americans survive and maintained confidence throughout the country. Its reforms increased the role of the federal government in the economic and social life of the nation. The government had become the regulator of Wall Street, the insurer of banks, and the provider of a modest amount of welfare. But it was World War II and its military purchases, not the New Deal, that pulled the U.S. economy out of the Great Depression.

REFORM OF THE FEDERAL JUDICIARY

. . . I want to talk with you very simply about the need for present action in this crisis—the need to meet the unanswered challenge of one-third of a nation ill-nourished, ill-clad, ill-housed.

Last Thursday I described the American form of government as a three-horse team provided by the Constitution to the American people so that their field might be plowed. The three horses are, of course, the three branches of government—the Congress, the executive, and the courts. Two of the horses are pulling in unison today; the third is not. Those who have intimated that the President of the United States is trying to drive that team overlook the simple fact that the President, as Chief Executive, is himself one of the three horses.

It is the American people themselves who are in the driver's seat.

It is the American people themselves who want the furrow plowed.

It is the American people themselves who expect the third horse to pull in unison with the other two. . . .

In the last 4 years the sound rule of giving statutes the benefit of all reasonable doubt has been cast aside. The Court has been acting not as a judicial body, but as a policy-making body.

When the Congress has sought to stabilize national agriculture, to improve the conditions of labor, to safeguard business against unfair competition, to protect our national resources, and in many other ways to serve our clearly national needs, the majority of the Court has been assuming the power to pass on the wisdom of these acts of the Congress—and to approve or disapprove the public policy written into these laws.

That is not only my accusation. It is the accusation of most distinguished Justices of the present Supreme Court. . . . But in the case holding the Railroad Retirement Act unconstitutional, for instance, Chief Justice Hughes said in a dissenting opinion that the majority opinion was "a departure from sound principles," and placed "an unwarranted limitation upon the commerce clause." And three other Justices agreed with him.

In the case holding the AAA unconstitutional, Justice Stone said of the majority opinion that it was a "tortured construction of the Constitution." And two other Justices agreed with him.

In the case holding the New York Minimum Wage Law unconstitutional, Justice Stone said that the majority were actually reading into the Constitution their own "personal economic predilections," and that if the legislative power is not left free to choose the methods of solving the problems of poverty, subsistence, and health of large numbers in the community, then "government is to be rendered impotent." And two other Justices agreed with him.

In the face of these dissenting opinions, there is no basis for the claim made by some members of the Court that something in the Constitution has compelled them regretfully to thwart the will of the people.

In the face of such dissenting opinions, it is perfectly clear that as Chief Justice Hughes has said, "We are under a Constitution, but the Constitution is what the judges say it is."

The Court in addition to the proper use of its judicial functions has improperly set itself up as a third House of the Congress—a super-legislature, as one of the Justices has called it—reading into the Constitution words and implications which are not there, and which were never intended to be there.

• *As the Supreme Court ruled some New Deal legislation unconstitutional, President Roosevelt became increasingly frustrated. On 5 February 1937, he proposed the Reform of the Federal Judiciary bill. His proposal to add six new justices to the Supreme Court was denounced as "court-packing."*

FOREIGN POLICY. Even in foreign policy, Roosevelt's priority was domestic economic recovery. Washington loosened its military presence in the Caribbean and resisted intervention in Mexican politics. The "Good Neighbor" policy, which had originated in the late 1920s, extended trade benefits throughout the Western Hemisphere.

Reflecting a national mood of isolationism, Congress had readily passed a series of neutrality acts to keep the United States out of "foreign wars." The first, enacted in 1935, provided that whenever the president proclaimed a state of war anywhere in the world, all shipments of arms to any warring countries, whether aggressor or victim, would cease. It also forbade the use of U.S. ships for transporting war material and warned Americans that they traveled on ships of countries at war at their own risk. In February 1936, a Second Neutrality Act prohibited U.S. bankers from lending money to countries at war (belligerents). Roosevelt, careful not to endanger his upcoming reelection, reluctantly signed the bills. In November 1939, a third act allowed belligerents to buy U.S. armaments only if they paid cash and transported them in their own ships—the "cash and carry" provision. This last legislation also forbade U.S. citizens and ships from entering any area designated a combat zone by the president.

When the Japanese sank the U.S. gunboat *Panay* in China in December 1937, Roosevelt was still leading a nation that favored neutrality. Convinced that the country would have to fight fascism, the President slowly turned the United States to face the possibility of intervention. He met with representatives of all republics of the Western Hemisphere at Panama in September 1939, and the resulting Declaration of Panama mapped out a war-free zone 300 miles out to sea from the neutral United States and pledged joint action in response to any threats.

Instead of outright intervention in the European war that broke out in September 1939, Roosevelt favored supplying Great Britain with weapons to use against Germany. Most Americans were coming to realize that the United States could no longer ignore the military threat posed by Germany, Japan, and Italy (the Axis powers). In August 1940 Congress passed the Selective Service Act, the first peacetime draft in U.S. history, which Congress extended in the summer of 1941 by only one vote.

As Germany expanded its air campaign against Great Britain, British Prime Minister Winston Churchill pleaded for additional aid from Roosevelt. Roosevelt convinced Congress to pass the Lend-Lease Act in 1941. It was intended to end the "cash and carry" provision of the 1939 Neutrality Act, which was blocking aid to an already bankrupt Great Britain. Roosevelt used terms understandable to every American in a fireside radio chat: "When your neighbor's house is on fire, you lend him your garden hose." He concluded that the Americas must be the "great arsenal of democracy." The President gave 50 old destroyers to Great Britain in exchange for long-term U.S. leases on military bases in Newfoundland, Bermuda, and islands in the Caribbean. This decision ended U.S. neutrality.

CAMPAIGN OF 1940. In the presidential campaign of 1940, Roosevelt faced Wendell L. Wilkie of Indiana, a liberal internationalist. Roosevelt assured Americans: "Your boys are not going to be sent into any foreign wars." He won reelection by a margin of nearly 5 million popular votes.

On 6 January 1941, in his State of the Union message, Roosevelt pledged the preservation of the Four Freedoms: freedom of speech, freedom of religion, freedom from want, and freedom from the fear of armed aggression. His address promised full support to the Allies. On 9 August 1941, Churchill met Roosevelt on a ship off the coast of Newfoundland and confirmed the Four Freedoms as a common goal in a joint statement known as the Atlantic Charter. Originally meant to rally supporters to the Allied forces, the charter became a blueprint for the postwar world. It also called for self-determination for all people, freedom of the seas, equal commercial opportunities, and disarmament. The two leaders demanded the

President Roosevelt was inaugurated for his third term on 20 January 1941 after an overwhelming victory over the Republican candidate, Wendell Wilkie. (Courtesy National Archives.)

disarmament of the Axis powers and a "permanent system of general security"—the future United Nations. Within a month, 15 countries, including the Soviet Union, had endorsed the Charter.

After repeated attacks by German submarines on U.S. vessels, Roosevelt pushed Congress to amend the Neutrality Act once again. This time it allowed the arming of U.S. merchant ships carrying cargoes to the ports of warring countries. The United States was now involved in the battle of the Atlantic, and public opinion gradually shifted toward aiding Great Britain.

In the Pacific, Roosevelt had maintained moderately courteous relations with Japan until 1938. But after that the United States gave more and more aid to the Chinese nationalist leader, Chiang Kai-shek, against both Mao Zedong's communist forces and the Japanese, who had bombed and invaded northern China. Following the Japanese surprise attack on the U.S. naval base at Pearl Harbor on 7 December 1941, the American public rallied behind Roosevelt. Congress declared war on Japan the following day. Very soon after that, Germany declared war on the United States. The President immediately set up the War Production Board to build a war industry by banning produc-

tion of nonessential goods and guaranteeing profits to certain businesses. In April 1942, the President created the War Manpower Commission to manage human resources.

In November 1943, Churchill, Roosevelt, and Joseph Stalin, the leader of the Soviet Union, met at Teheran, Iran. The three rulers agreed on the postwar partition of Germany, on the need to create a United Nations peacekeeping body, and on a

Marshal Joseph Stalin (left), President Franklin D. Roosevelt, and Prime Minister Winston Churchill (right) met together for the first time in Teheran, Iran on 28 November 1943. Stalin announced at this meeting that the U.S.S.R. would join the war against Japan as soon as Germany was defeated. (Courtesy National Archives.)

plan for the joint administration of each liberated country until new democratic governments could be elected. The Allied invasion of Europe was discussed at this meeting.

ELECTION OF 1944. Amid the disorder of World War II, Roosevelt ran for a fourth term in 1944, substituting Senator Harry S. Truman of Missouri for Henry A. Wallace as his vice presidential running mate. The Republicans named Governor Thomas E. Dewey of New York as their presidential nominee. During the campaign, Roosevelt's weak health, his vision of the postwar world, and his right to run for an unprecedented fourth term were debated. Using "don't change horses in midstream" as his campaign slogan, Roosevelt once again won an easy reelection.

In order to prepare for postwar monetary stability and healthy international trade, Roosevelt organized a conference at Bretton Woods, New Hampshire in July 1944. It brought together delegates from most of the Allied nations. Secretary of the Treasury Henry Morgenthau chaired the meeting which made plans to establish the International Monetary Fund (IMF) and the International Bank for Reconstruction and Development (IBRD). Continuing to prepare for the postwar world, Roosevelt, Churchill, and Stalin met again at Yalta, U.S.S.R., in February 1945 and agreed on the reconstruction of eastern Europe and Germany. They scheduled a confer-

THE ATLANTIC CHARTER

The President of the United States of America and the Prime Minister, Mr. Churchill, representing His Majesty's Government in the United Kingdom, being met together, deem it right to make known certain common principles in the national policies of their respective countries on which they base their hopes for a better future for the world.

First, their countries seek no aggrandizement (greater power), territorial or other;

Second, they desire to see no territorial changes that do not accord with the freely expressed wishes of the peoples concerned;

Third, they respect the right of all peoples to choose the form of government under which they will live; and they wish to see sovereign rights and self government restored to those who have been forcibly deprived of them;

Fourth, they will endeavor, with due respect for their existing obligations, to further the enjoyment by all States, great or small, victor or vanquished, of access, on equal terms, to the trade and to the raw materials of the world which are needed for their economic prosperity;

Fifth, they desire to bring about the fullest collaboration between all nations in the economic field with the object of securing, for all, improved labor standards, economic advancement and social security;

Sixth, after the final destruction of the Nazi tyranny, they hope to see established a peace which will afford to all nations the means of dwelling in safety within their own boundaries, and which will afford assurance that all the men in all the lands may live out their lives in freedom from fear and want;

Seventh, such a peace should enable all men to traverse the high seas and oceans without hindrance;

Eighth, they believe that all of the nations of the world, for realistic as well as spiritual reasons must come to the abandonment of the use of force. Since no future peace can be maintained if land, sea or air armaments continue to be employed by nations which threaten, or may threaten, aggression outside of their frontiers, they believe, pending the establishment of a wider and permanent system of general security, that the disarmament of such nations is essential. They will likewise aid and encourage all other practicable measures which will lighten for peace-loving peoples the crushing burden of armaments.

• *President Franklin D. Roosevelt and Prime Minister Winston Churchill signed the Atlantic Charter in August 1941 at Placentia Bay off Newfoundland. The British did not get as much of a military commitment as they had wished. In* FDR: A Biography, *historian Ted Morgan wrote, "The meeting was a success in personal terms, however, the start of a friendship based on Churchill's side on equal parts of dire need and genuine fondness."*

REQUEST FOR DECLARATION OF WAR

Yesterday, December 7, 1941—a date which will live in infamy—the United States of America was suddenly and deliberately attacked by naval and air forces of the Empire of Japan.

The United States was at peace with that nation and, at the solicitation of Japan, was still in conversation with its Government and its Emperor looking toward the maintenance of peace in the Pacific. Indeed, one hour after Japanese air squadrons had commenced bombing in Oahu, the Japanese Ambassador to the United States and his colleague delivered to the Secretary of State a formal reply to a recent American message. While this reply stated that it seemed useless to continue the existing diplomatic negotiations, it contained no threat or hint of war or armed attack.

It will be recorded that the distance of Hawaii from Japan makes it obvious that the attack was deliberately planned many days or even weeks ago. During the intervening time the Japanese Government has deliberately sought to deceive the United States by false statements and expressions of hope for continued peace.

The attack yesterday on the Hawaiian Islands has caused severe damage to American naval and military forces. Very many American lives have been lost. In addition American ships have been reported torpedoed on the high seas between San Francisco and Honolulu.

Yesterday the Japanese Government also launched an attack against Malaya. Last night Japanese forces attacked Hong Kong. Last night Japanese forces attacked Guam. Last night Japanese forces attacked the Philippine Islands. Last night the Japanese attacked Wake Island. This morning the Japanese attacked Midway Island.

Japan has, therefore, undertaken a surprise offensive extending throughout the Pacific area. The facts of yesterday speak for themselves. The people of the United States have already formed their opinions and well understand the implications to the very life and safety of our nation.

As Commander-in-Chief of the Army and Navy, I have directed that all measures be taken for our defense.

Always will be remembered the character of the onslaught against us.

No matter how long it may take us to overcome this premeditated invasion, the American people in their righteous might will win through to absolute victory.

I believe I interpret the will of the Congress and of the people when I assert that we will not only defend ourselves to the uttermost but will make very certain that this form of treachery shall never endanger us again.

Hostilities exist. There is no blinking at the fact that our people, our territory and our interests are in grave danger.

With confidence in our armed forces—with the unbounding determination of our people—we will gain the inevitable triumph—so help us God.

I ask that the Congress declare that since the unprovoked and dastardly attack by Japan on Sunday, December seventh, a state of war has existed between the United States and the Japanese Empire.

• *On 8 December 1941, President Roosevelt asked Congress for a declaration of war against Japan. A state of war was declared in 33 minutes.*

President Roosevelt signed the Declaration of War against Japan on 8 December 1941. Only one member of the House, Jeanette Rankin, cast a dissenting vote. Roosevelt was wearing a black arm band in memory of his mother who had died earlier that year. (Courtesy Library of Congress.)

ence for April 1945 in San Francisco to work out the institutional arrangement for a future United Nations. In a joint declaration, they restated their belief in self-determination to all countries.

DEATH. Roosevelt did not live to see the end of the war. He died in Warm Springs, Georgia on 12 April 1945 of a massive cerebral hemorrhage. His legacy shaped the rest of twentieth-century America. Governing for more than 12 years, through depression and war, he had strengthened executive power and greatly furthered the involvement of the federal government in the social and economic lives of all Americans. Roosevelt also moved the country from isolationism to internationalism. As the war grew closer to America's shores, the President—strongly influenced by Theodore Roosevelt's balance-of-power-realism and Woodrow Wilson's idealistic vision of an organized world peace—cautiously prepared the nation for leadership in the postwar world.

Elizabeth Shoumatoff was painting this portrait of President Roosevelt in the Little White House on 12 April 1945. The President raised his hand to his head and said, "I have a terrific headache" and slumped in his chair. He was pronounced dead at 3:35 P.M. (Courtesy Parks and Historic Sites Division, Georgia Department of Natural Resources.)

VICE PRESIDENT

John Nance Garner
(1868–1967)

CHRONOLOGICAL EVENTS

1868	Born, Detroit, Texas, 22 November
1892	Elected judge of Uvalde County, Texas
1898	Elected to Texas House of Representatives
1902	Elected to U.S. House of Representatives
1931	Elected Speaker of the House
1932	Elected vice president
1967	Died, Uvalde, Texas, 7 November

BIOGRAPHY

John Nance Garner divided his long life between the tiny Texas town of Uvalde and the corridors of power in Washington. Growing up on the Texas frontier, he went to the University of Tennessee. Poor grades and poor health sent him back to read law in Texas. Moving to Uvalde for its dry climate, Garner served first as a judge and then as a member of the Texas legislature. While chairing a congressional redistricting committee, he created the district in which he ran for the U.S. House of Representatives in 1902. "Cactus Jack" Garner spent the next 30 years in the House.

The stock market crash of 1929 returned the Democrats to the majority in the House and elevated Garner to Speaker. As the nation slid into the Depression, Speaker Garner rejected President Herbert Hoover's cautious programs and proposed massive federal aid to the unemployed. He became a leading contender for the Democratic nomination for president in 1932. When the nomination went instead to New York Governor Franklin D. Roosevelt, Garner reluctantly agreed to run for vice president. He was reelected to his House seat at the same time he won the vice presidency.

During Garner's last months as Speaker, Roosevelt solicited his advice about legislation. When Garner shifted to presiding over the U.S. Senate, he continued to advise Roosevelt on legislative tactics. Avoiding speech making, social entertaining, and official travel, Garner thrived on backroom political maneuvering. But as Roosevelt's New Deal shifted steadily to the left, the more conservative vice president felt his influence decline within the administration. Before long, Garner complained that the vice presidency was "not worth a bucket of warm spit."

After Roosevelt and Garner won a landslide reelection in 1936, the President announced a dramatic plan to increase the size of the Supreme Court. Critics accused Roosevelt of trying to "pack" the Court to prevent it from overturning New Deal laws. Although Garner never spoke against the plan, he clearly demonstrated his opposition. During the Senate debate, the Vice President suddenly left the capital to go fishing in Texas. Roosevelt took this as an act of disloyalty.

As the 1940 election approached, Garner joined those Democrats who wanted to stop Roosevelt from running for a third term. But at the convention, Garner trailed far behind Roosevelt. President Roosevelt then chose Henry Wallace for vice president. Garner returned home without bothering to vote in the election. He remained in Uvalde until his death at age 98.

VICE PRESIDENT

Henry Agard Wallace
(1888–1965)

CHRONOLOGICAL EVENTS

1888	Born, Orient, Iowa, 7 October
1910	Graduated from Iowa State College, Ames, Iowa
1921	Editor, *Wallace's Farmer* Magazine
1933	Appointed secretary of agriculture
1940	Elected vice president
1945	Appointed secretary of commerce
1948	Ran unsuccessfully for president
1965	Died, Danbury, Connecticut, 18 November

BIOGRAPHY

Grandson of the founder of a popular agricultural journal, *Wallace's Farmer*, and son of a secretary of agriculture, Henry Wallace felt more at home farming than engaged in politics. Raised in Iowa, Wallace studied plant genetics at Iowa State College. He later patented and marketed a high-yielding hybrid corn.

When his father joined President Warren G. Harding's cabinet in 1921, Wallace took over editing the family magazine. He broke with the Republican Party over its farm policies and supported the Democrats in 1932. President Franklin D. Roosevelt then named him secretary of agriculture. In the cabinet, Wallace promoted such innovations as financial subsidies for farmers, crop and livestock limitations to reduce supply and raise prices, food stamps, and school lunch programs.

Idealistic and energetic, Wallace traveled widely to speak for New Deal liberalism. He endorsed a third term for Roosevelt in 1940. When Republicans nominated a popular farm state senator for vice president, Roosevelt chose Wallace as his running mate, despite his lack of experience in elective office. Some Democrats protested, but Roosevelt warned that he would not run again if they rejected Wallace.

Wallace felt out of place among the politicians on Capitol Hill. Seeking to make better use of his talents, President Roosevelt broke precedent to give his vice president executive responsibilities. During World War II, Wallace chaired the Economic Defense Board, the Supply Priorities and Allocations Board, and the Board of Economic Warfare. Roosevelt also sent Wallace on missions to Latin America, China, and the Soviet Union.

Fearful that Roosevelt might not survive a fourth term, key Democratic leaders were determined that Wallace should not succeed him. Using polls that showed Democrats overwhelmingly opposed to Wallace, they convinced Roosevelt to let them nominate Missouri Senator Harry S. Truman for vice president. To compensate, Roosevelt appointed Wallace secretary of commerce.

Roosevelt's death made Truman president. When Wallace called for greater cooperation with the Soviet Union, Truman fired him for differing with his cold war policies. Wallace edited *The New Republic* magazine briefly before running as the Progressive Party candidate against Truman in 1948. Soundly defeated, he retired from politics to raise corn on his farm in Connecticut.

VICE PRESIDENT

Harry S. Truman
(1884–1972)

CHRONOLOGICAL EVENTS

1884	Born, Lamar, Missouri, 8 May
1917	Enlisted in the U.S. Army
1922	Elected judge of Jackson County, Missouri
1934	Elected to U.S. Senate
1944	Elected vice president
1945	Became president upon the death of Franklin D. Roosevelt
1948	Elected president
1972	Died, Kansas City, Missouri, 26 December

BIOGRAPHY

Harry S. Truman spent his childhood on his grandmother's farm in Missouri. Because of his father's bankruptcy, Truman could not attend college. He worked at several jobs before going back to run the family farm.

During World War I, Truman abandoned farming to serve as captain in a National Guard unit in Europe. He returned to marry his childhood sweetheart, Bess Wallace, and moved into her home in Independence, Missouri.

Truman operated a men's clothing store that failed during the recession of 1922. He turned for help to Thomas Pendergast, boss of the Kansas City Democratic machine. With Pendergast's endorsement, Truman was elected county judge of Jackson County, where he established a strong record. In 1934, Pendergast backed Truman for the U.S. Senate. Working diligently as a senator, Truman generally supported Franklin D. Roosevelt's New Deal. After Pendergast went to prison for tax evasion in 1939, Truman won a tough race for renomination and reelection.

During World War II, he received national publicity for chairing the "Truman Committee," a special committee to investigate the national defense program. Its efforts to root out fraud in defense contracting propelled Truman to the Democratic nomination for vice president in 1944.

Meeting with Roosevelt after his nomination, Truman was shocked at the President's sickly appearance. Yet even after their election, he rarely saw Roosevelt and received little information from him. He learned nothing about the secret plans to develop atomic weapons. As presiding officer of the Senate, Truman regretted losing his right to speak and vote, except to cast one tie-breaking vote. When he finished presiding on the afternoon of 12 April 1945, Truman walked to the "Board of Education," a room in the House wing of the Capitol where Speaker Sam Rayburn's friends gathered to relax. A telephone message summoned Truman to the White House. There Eleanor Roosevelt informed him that the President had died of a cerebral hemorrhage.

Largely unprepared for the presidency, Truman struggled with postwar economic conversion and with the growing cold war tensions between the United States with the Soviet Union. Republicans took control of Congress in 1946 and seemed destined to recapture the White House in 1948. Truman surprised them by waging an aggressive "give-'em-hell" campaign and won an upset victory.

THE CABINET

SECRETARY OF STATE
Cordell Hull, 1933, 1937, 1941
Edward R. Stettinius, Jr., 1944, 1945

SECRETARY OF WAR
George H. Dren, 1933
Harry H. Woodring, 1937
Henry L. Stimson, 1940, 1941, 1945

SECRETARY OF THE TREASURY
W.H. Woodin, 1933
Henry Morgenthau, Jr., 1934, 1937, 1941, 1945

POSTMASTER GENERAL
James A. Farley, 1933, 1937
Frank C. Walker, 1940, 1941, 1945

ATTORNEY GENERAL
Homer S. Cummings, 1933, 1937
Frank Murphy, 1939
Robert H. Jackson, 1940, 1941
Francis Biddle, 1941, 1945

SECRETARY OF THE NAVY
Claude A. Swanson, 1933, 1937
Charles Edison, 1939, 1940
Frank Knox, 1940
James V. Forrestal, 1944, 1945

SECRETARY OF THE INTERIOR
Harold L. Ickes, 1933, 1937, 1941, 1945

SECRETARY OF AGRICULTURE
Henry A. Wallace, 1933, 1937
Claude R. Wickard, 1940, 1941, 1945

SECRETARY OF COMMERCE
Daniel C. Roper, 1933, 1937
Harry L. Hopkins, 1938, 1939
Jesse H. Jones, 1940, 1941, 1945
Henry A. Wallace, 1945

SECRETARY OF LABOR
Frances Perkins, 1933, 1937, 1941, 1945

(Courtesy U.S. Army; Dwight D. Eisenhower Library.)

James V. Forrestal (1892–1949). Forrestal was appointed secretary of the navy by President Franklin D. Roosevelt in 1944. After the death of President Roosevelt, he retained his post in the administration of Harry S. Truman. He had previously served as undersecretary of the navy.

As secretary of the navy, Forrestal advised President Truman to change the doctrine of unconditional surrender to allow the Emperor of Japan to remain as nominal (existing in name only) sovereign. He also persuaded Truman to establish a permanent U.S. naval presence in the Pacific and in the Mediterranean. He was the only cabinet officer to oppose the use of the atomic bomb on Japan without prior warning.

At first, Forrestal opposed Truman's proposal to unify the army, navy, and air force under a single Department of Defense. After the passage of the National Security Act of 1947, which secured a degree of independence between the army, navy, and air force, he accepted appointment as the first secretary of defense in July of that year.

In March 1949, Forrestal resigned when he was unable to solve interservice problems that had developed due to the unification.

FAMILY

CHRONOLOGICAL EVENTS

11 October 1884	(Anna) Eleanor Roosevelt born	17 August 1914	Son, Franklin D., Jr., born
17 March 1905	Eleanor Roosevelt married	13 March 1916	Son, John Aspinwall, born
	Franklin Delano Roosevelt	12 April 1945	Franklin Delano Roosevelt
3 May 1906	Daughter, Anna Eleanor, born		died
23 December 1907	Son, James, born	7 November 1962	Eleanor Roosevelt died
23 September 1910	Son, Elliott, born		

◀ *This striking portrait of Eleanor Roosevelt was taken by the famous photographer, Fabian Bachrach, in 1940, in the Monroe room of the White House. Mrs. Roosevelt is standing beneath a portrait of her grandfather.* (Courtesy Library of Congress.)

Eleanor Roosevelt was a distant cousin of Franklin D. Roosevelt. They were both descended from Claes Martenszen van Roosevelt, who arrived in New Amsterdam from Holland in the 1640s. They were married at her aunt's home, and she was given away by her uncle, President Theodore Roosevelt.

She once said that she feared that she was going to become a prisoner in the White House "with nothing to do except stand in line and receive visitors and preside over official dinners." However, she was one of the most active First Ladies in history, and she remained active until her death. Her biographer, Joseph P. Lash, said that she served as a "listening post" for her husband so that "he obtained a balanced picture of what the country was thinking and feeling." She became the voice for those who had no voice—the working men and women, the poor and the needy, and the African American.

Eleanor Roosevelt delivered the commencement address at Columbia University in 1948 and met with Dwight D. Eisenhower who was president of the university then. President Harry S. Truman appointed her to the first U.S. delegation to the United Nations where she served from 1946 to 1952. President John F. Kennedy reappointed her to that position in 1961. She died in 1962. (Courtesy Dwight D. Eisenhower Library.) ▶

All four Roosevelt sons served in the armed forces during World War II. (Clockwise from top left) Elliott had an excellent record in the Army Air Force. After flying in North Africa and the Mediterranean, he was put in charge of a photo reconnaissance unit involved in the preparation for D-Day. He was awarded the Distinguished Flying Cross and was discharged a brigadier general. Elliott later edited a four-volume edition of his father's letters. He also wrote a controversial book about the family which the other Roosevelt children did not like, and several murder mysteries.

James Roosevelt joined the Marine Corps in 1940 and chose combat duty after the attack on Pearl Harbor. He served in the Pacific including the attack on Makin Island. He was awarded the Navy Cross and the Silver Star. James lost the 1950 election for the governor of California and served 11 years in the U.S. House of Representatives.

John graduated from Harvard University and served with the U.S. Navy from 1941 to 1946 and was discharged a lieutenant commander. He became a Republican and was chairman of Citizens for Eisenhower.

Franklin D., Jr. graduated from Harvard University and earned a law degree from the

(Courtesy Franklin D. Roosevelt Library.)

University of Virginia in 1940. He was on active duty with the U.S. Navy from 1941 to 1945 and became a lieutenant commander. He was awarded the Purple Heart and the Silver Star. He was elected to the U.S. House of Representatives in 1949. He later served as undersecretary of commerce during the Kennedy and Johnson administrations.

When the President died, Mrs. Roosevelt cabled her sons: "He did his job to the end as he would want you to do."

Anna was the Roosevelts' eldest child and only daughter. At FDR's request, she moved into the White House and remained there until his death. She was one of the President's closest companions, and she acted as the White House hostess during her mother's frequent absences. Anna accompanied the President to the Yalta Conference in 1945.

◀ Anna Roosevelt is shown here with her parents in October 1932 driving from the train station to their home in Warm Springs, Georgia. (Courtesy Franklin D. Roosevelt Library.)

HOME OF FRANKLIN D. ROOSEVELT NATIONAL HISTORIC SITE

Albany Post Road
Hyde Park, New York 12538
(914) 229-9115

The first floor of the mansion contains Roosevelt's office, used as his Summer White House. From this room, on 6 November 1944, he broadcast his last campaign speech. (Courtesy Franklin D. Roosevelt Library.)

Located approximately 70 miles north of New York on New York Route 9, near Poughkeepsie. Open daily, April through October, from 9 A.M. to 5 P.M. Closed Tuesdays and Wednesdays from November through March. Admission fee. Young adults 17 and under and adults 62 and over admitted free. Administered by the National Park Service, U.S. Department of the Interior.

Franklin D. Roosevelt was born in a 30-room mansion at Hyde Park on 30 January 1882. He spent most of his life there, from childhood through raising his five children with his wife, Eleanor, on to launching his political career—which stretched from the New York State Senate to the White House.

The central part of the building dates back to the 1800s. It has undergone several renovations, inclu-

ding a front porch with columns, and a two-story wing addition on each end. In 1944, the house and grounds were designated a National Historic Site. The 33-acre estate then consisted of the home, outer buildings, and the gravesite. It now contains 188 acres and a library. The formal dedication ceremony took place on 12 April 1946, the first anniversary of Roosevelt's death.

FRANKLIN D. ROOSEVELT LIBRARY AND MUSEUM

259 Albany Post Road • Hyde Park, New York 12538 • Tel: (914) 229-8114

Located a few hundred feet from the Home of Franklin D. Roosevelt National Historic Site. Open daily from 9 A.M. to 5 P.M. Closed Thanksgiving, Christmas, and New Year's Day. One admission fee charged for entrance to both the library-museum and the mansion. Administered by the National Archives and Records Service.

The library section contains nearly 40,000 books (including Roosevelt's 15,000-volume personal library), manuscripts and documents totaling more than 15 million pages, and pictorial collections. The museum section contains the president's study, his ship models, personal gifts from foreign rulers, and exhibits that highlight the lives and careers of Roosevelt and his wife, Eleanor. The library was dedicated on 30 June 1941.

At the dedication ceremony, President Roosevelt stated: "It seems to me that the dedication of a library is in itself an act of faith, to bring together the records of the past and to house them in buildings where they will be preserved for the use of men and women in the future. A nation must believe in—in three things.
It must believe in the past.
It must believe in the future.
It must, above all, believe in the capacity of its own people so to learn from the past that they can gain in judgment in creating their own future." (Courtesy Franklin D. Roosevelt Library)

LITTLE WHITE HOUSE

Route 1 • P.O. Box 10 • Warm Springs, Georgia 31830 • Tel: (404) 655-3511

Located off Georgia Route 85W and U.S. Route 27. Open daily. Hours are seasonal; call for times. Closed Thanksgiving and Christmas. Admission fee. The site contains a museum, a gift shop, a snack bar, and picnic grounds. The 10,000-acre Franklin D. Roosevelt State Park is located nearby. The home and park are operated by the Georgia Department of Natural Resources, Division of Parks, Recreation and Historic Parks.

The Little White House is furnished with FDR's mementos, paintings, and personal items. (Courtesy Parks and Historic Sites Division, Georgia Department of Natural Resources.)

In 1924, Roosevelt visited Warm Springs searching for relief from polio. He found the warm mineral-spring waters rejuvenating, and soon had plans drawn for the Little White House. Completed in the spring of 1932, the six-room country home was built on the north slope of Pine Mountain. News of Roosevelt's improvement encouraged hundreds of polio victims to go to Warm Springs, Georgia. The Georgia Warm Springs Foundation was established, and Roosevelt chose architect Henry J. Toombs to plan the treatment center and public pool. For the next 21 years, Roosevelt was closely tied to the springs. The home remains substantially as it was when he died of a stroke there in 1945.

ROOSEVELT CAMPOBELLO INTERNATIONAL PARK

P.O. Box 9 • Welshpool, New Brunswick E0G 3H0 • Canada • Tel: (506) 752-2922

Located at the southeastern end of Canadian island of Campobello, near the Maine–New Brunswick border. Principal access to the island is the Franklin D. Roosevelt Memorial Bridge at Lubec, Maine. Take U.S. 1 to State 189. Open daily, 27 May through 9 October, from 9 A.M. to 5 P.M. No admission fee. Tours available. Handicapped accessible. The site contains the Roosevelt Cottage, other tour cottages, walking trails, picnic areas, beaches, gift shops, and a visitor center. For more information, write: Executive Secretary, P.O. Box 97, Lubec, ME 04652. Funded by the federal governments of the United States and Canada. Administered by an International Park Commission with equal representation from both countries.

In 1883, Roosevelt's father, James, purchased four acres and a partially completed house on Campobello Island. Two years later, the house was completed. This house, which became known as Granny's Cottage, is located north of the present Roosevelt Cottage—which Roosevelt's mother, Sara, purchased in 1910, and later gave to Franklin and Eleanor as a wedding gift.

In 1964, the Roosevelt Campobello International Park was established under an agreement signed by President Lyndon B. Johnson and Canadian Prime Minister Lester B. Pearson. The 2,800-acre park was officially opened on 20 August 1964. In 1966, the cornerstone of the new visitor center was laid. The 34-room Roosevelt Cottage contains most of the furnishings used by the Roosevelt family, including Franklin's crib, his collection of canes, and the family telescope. The wallpaper, curtains, and rugs are originals, or reproductions provided by the Park Commission.

◄ *Roosevelt spent almost every summer on the island between 1883, when he was one year old, and 1921, when he was stricken with polio. Nearly 12 years passed before he was able to return to Campobello.* (Courtesy Roosevelt Campobello International Park Commission.)

The Visitor Center of the Roosevelt Campobello International Park was officially opened by Queen Elizabeth on 13 July 1967. At the opening ceremony, she said: "It is most fitting that the memory of so gallant and illustrious an American should be honoured on the Canadian Island which he loved."
(Courtesy Roosevelt Campobello International Park Commission.) ►

Harry S. Truman

CHRONOLOGICAL EVENTS

8 May 1884	Born, Lamar, Missouri
1901	Graduated from high school
1903	Bank clerk, Kansas City, Missouri
1917–1919	Served in World War I; commanded Battery D, 129th Field Artillery
7 November 1922	Elected county judge of eastern district, Jackson County, Missouri
2 November 1926	Elected presiding judge, Jackson County, Missouri
6 November 1934	Elected to U.S. Senate
5 November 1940	Reelected to U.S. Senate
1941	Appointed chairman of Senate Committee to Investigate the National Defense Program
7 November 1944	Elected vice president
12 April 1945	Became president upon the death of Franklin D. Roosevelt
8 May 1945	Announced surrender of Germany
6 August 1945	Atomic bomb dropped on Hiroshima, Japan
9 August 1945	Second atomic bomb dropped on Nagasaki, Japan
14 August 1945	Announced surrender of Japan
12 March 1947	Issued Truman Doctrine
April 1948	Marshall Plan (European Recovery Program) approved
24 June 1948	Berlin Blockade
2 November 1948	Elected president
20 January 1949	Inaugurated president
4 April 1949	North Atlantic Treaty Organization (NATO) founded
27 June 1950	Dispatched U.S. troops to South Korea
22 September 1950	Vetoed Internal Security Act (The McCarran Act)
11 April 1951	Relieved General Douglas MacArthur of Far East command
8 April 1952	Seized steel mills to prevent strike
29 March 1952	Announced that he would not run for reelection
20 January 1953	Retired to Independence, Missouri
1956	Published memoirs, *Years of Trial and Hope*
26 December 1972	Died, Kansas City, Missouri

BIOGRAPHY

Harry S. Truman became president of the United States at one of the most critical times in history. Almost completely unprepared for his global responsibilities, he managed to cope with them by means of his intellect, integrity, and political skill. He served almost two full terms. Most historians agree that he did an impressive job in both. The great British Prime Minister Winston Churchill told him, "You more than any other man have saved Western civilization."

YOUTH. Truman was born on 8 May 1884 in the small town of Lamar, Missouri. The oldest son of John Truman, a livestock trader, and Martha Young, he spent his early childhood in the farm country of western Missouri. When he was six, his parents moved to the large town of Independence, so that he could get a good public school education. Because he was farsighted and read a lot, he often wore thick glasses in childhood. He did well in school, where history was his favorite subject. He also became a good piano player.

Truman graduated from high school in 1901. In that year, his father lost all his money in a bad investment and was unable to send him to college. Truman took a series of jobs in nearby Kansas City—in a newspaper mailroom, in railroad construction, and in a bank. In 1905, when his father needed him to help on the family farm, he had to leave Kansas City. He spent the next 11 years as a farmer.

WORLD WAR I. In 1917, the United States entered World War I. Truman was in his early thirties, well past the military draft age. Nevertheless, he was so stirred by the idealistic speeches of President Woodrow Wilson that he volunteered for the U.S. Army. He served until 1919, rising from lieutenant to major. He commanded an artillery unit in the fierce battles of 1918 in France. Truman was an effective officer who was also popular with his men. The war was a turning point for him, because it took him away from the farm and proved to him that he could be a leader.

LOCAL POLITICS. After the war, Truman returned to Kansas City and opened a men's clothing store. He also married his childhood sweetheart from Independence, Bess Wallace. The store failed after two years, but during that time Truman caught the attention of the powerful Democratic political

▲ *Harry S. Truman married Bess Wallace on 28 June 1919 in Independence, Missouri. They had known each other since they met as children in Sunday school.* (Courtesy Harry S. Truman Library.)

▲ *Harry S. Truman was a captain in the 129th Field Artillery when this picture was taken in France in July 1918.* (Courtesy Harry S. Truman Library.)

machine in Kansas City that was run by T. J. (Tom) Pendergast. The Pendergast organization, typical for its time, controlled the city government by a mixture of corruption and political favors. In order to present a decent image to voters, it needed respectable candidates for public offices. Truman, a loyal Democrat, was ideal for the Pendergast machine because he was honest, capable, interested in politics, and popular.

With the help of the machine, Truman was elected to important offices in Jackson County, which included Kansas City. From 1922 to 1924, he was the judge (county commissioner) for the eastern part of the county. From 1926 to 1934, he was the presiding judge (county executive). As an official, he was a success. He supported improved roads and public buildings without spending lavishly. He was a poor speaker and lacked an exciting personality, but people voted for him because of his character and ability. Although loyal to the Pendergast machine until its collapse around 1940, he never took part in its corrupt activities.

U.S. SENATOR. In 1934, the political machine chose Truman to run for the U. S. Senate. He was elected easily. Once he was in the Senate, he supported the New Deal policies of President Franklin D. Roosevelt, but he was not personally close to him. In fact, when Truman ran for reelection in 1940, Roosevelt gave him only lukewarm support. At about the same time, the Pendergast machine broke down, making this election the closest of his career. He won by campaigning tirelessly.

As World War II raged in Europe, the Senate Democrats chose Truman to head a committee to investigate the national defense program. His service on the Truman Committee made him famous. Even before the United States entered the war in December 1941, the committee uncovered a great amount of waste and carelessness in defense spending. When the United States did enter the war, his committee's work in saving money was even more important. By 1943, a poll of journalists named Truman as one of the 10 men in Washington who were doing the most to help win the war.

VICE PRESIDENT. By 1944, several leading Democrats were dissatisfied with Vice President Henry A. Wallace. They felt that he was not qualified to be president. Because of Roosevelt's failing health, they wanted to replace Wallace on the Democratic ticket. After considering several possibilities with Roosevelt, they finally selected Truman. The choice was made without his knowledge, but he accepted when told of Roosevelt's wishes. In November, Roosevelt and Truman were elected without difficulty. Five months later, on 12 April 1945, Roosevelt died of a stroke.

WORLD WAR II. Truman took office as World War II was ending. In Europe, Nazi Germany was almost defeated. American, British, Canadian, and Soviet troops were advancing on Hitler's headquarters from both east and west. No final decisions had been made about how to treat Germany or the countries it had conquered in Eastern Europe after the war.

Germany surrendered on 7 May. In the Pacific, Japan showed no signs of surrendering although they had been forced back to their own islands. The problem in the Pacific was how to defeat Japan as quickly as possible and bring the war to an end.

Shortly after taking office, Truman learned about the Manhattan Project, a scientific and military project that had almost completed the development of an atomic bomb. The greatest weapon of mass destruction in history, it would give the United States a significant advantage in the war against Japan. It might even persuade the Japanese to surrender. In July 1945, the atom bomb, still a secret, was successfully tested in New Mexico. Truman authorized its use against one or more Japanese targets. On 6 August, the city of Hiroshima was largely destroyed by the first atomic bomb. The second atomic bomb was dropped on Nagasaki on 9 August. Japan surrendered five days later and World War II was over at long last. Truman's decision to use the atomic bomb twice on civilian populations is still hotly debated more than 50 years later.

POSTWAR POLICIES. Roosevelt had already made some plans for U.S. policy after the war, and

Truman tried to follow these faithfully. For instance, he gave the full support of the United States to the founding of the United Nations. It was formally chartered in San Francisco in 1945 and permanently headquartered in New York in 1950. Truman did as Roosevelt had done in discussing the future of Germany and Europe. In July 1945, he met with the leaders of the two most important allies—Winston Churchill of Great Britain, and Joseph Stalin of the Soviet Union. Their meeting was in Potsdam, outside the ruined German capital of Berlin.

The Potsdam Conference was held in the summer of 1945, after the defeat of Nazi Germany. Prime Minister Winston Churchill, Great Britain (left), and Marshal Joseph Stalin, the Soviet Union (right), agreed on very little. Stalin and Truman never met again. (U.S. Army, Courtesy Harry S. Truman Library.)

The Potsdam Conference was not a success. Even before they met, Truman had learned that the Soviets were not keeping agreements they had previously made with Roosevelt. The Soviet Union was a communist state with a government-run economy and strict control over its citizens. It was setting up similar governments rather than democratic ones in Eastern Europe. It had taken a large part of German territory and given it to Poland. Stalin refused to discuss these actions at Potsdam. All that was accomplished at Potsdam was the division of the remaining part of Germany into four occupation zones and agreement on the disarming of Germany. The three leaders also agreed that trials of war criminals would be held.

THE COLD WAR. Truman and Stalin never met again, yet relations between the United States and the Soviet Union became the most important matter of Truman's presidency. Like many other Americans, he had hoped that U.S.–Soviet cooperation during the war would lead to a peaceful, open world after the defeat of Germany and Japan. Instead, during 1945 and 1946, the Soviets stationed many of their troops in Eastern European countries and refused to withdraw troops from Iran. They supported a communist faction in China which was at war with the government. They also tried by political means to increase their influence in countries like France and Italy.

They limited communication between the areas they controlled and the rest of the world. As Churchill put it, an "Iron Curtain" had descended across the middle of Europe. In 1946, not long after the end of the war, the arrest of a spy in Canada revealed that the Soviets had been spying on the United States, particularly the U.S. nuclear program.

The Soviets were trying to take advantage of postwar disorder so that they could extend their control over neighboring countries. The question was whether the United States should oppose these efforts. Some of Truman's advisers, like the diplomat George Kennan and the talented young lawyer, Clark Clifford, quickly concluded that it should. Kennan argued that Russia had always been an aggressive power and that it desired world domination. Only the United States had the means to resist it. Clifford, in a report to Truman in July 1946, pointed to the growing military strength of the Soviets, even

Prime Minister Winston Churchill first referred to the "Iron Curtain" in a speech at Westminster College in Fulton, Missouri on 5 March 1946. The Soviet Union blamed Truman for sponsoring the speech. (Courtesy Library of Congress.)

though the war was over. He also referred to their delaying a final peace treaty in order to give themselves an excuse for more military growth.

Others in the government, like Secretary of State James F. Byrnes and the President himself, were slow in accepting this idea. Some, like former Vice President Henry A. Wallace (now secretary of commerce), refused to accept it at all. Truman had made up his mind by the end of 1946. He decided that the United States would try to resist Soviet advances into other countries. Wallace still disagreed, and Truman dismissed him from the cabinet.

The new U.S. policy was one of containment. Its aim was to prevent Soviet control from spreading over any more countries. It was not a policy of trying to take away control that the Soviets already had. Its first two important measures, both begun in 1947, were the Truman Doctrine and the Marshall Plan.

THE TRUMAN DOCTRINE. The Truman Doctrine was a response to a communist military force that was trying to overthrow the government of Greece. Specifically, it consisted of U.S. military aid, in the form of $400 million to Greece and its neighbor Turkey. Truman made the general policy clear in March 1947 when he asked Congress for the money. The policy was that the United States would give aid to any free country that was trying to resist an armed takeover. The United States would not tolerate military aggression against neighboring countries. Congress appropriated the money, and the Greek Government was not overthrown.

THE MARSHALL PLAN. In the summer of 1947,

THE TRUMAN DOCTRINE

. . . At the present moment in world history nearly every nation must choose between alternative ways of life. The choice is too often not a free one.

One way of life is based upon the will of the majority, and is distinguished by free institutions, representative government, free elections, guarantees of individual liberty, freedom of speech and religion, and freedom from political oppression.

The second way of life is based upon the will of the minority forcibly imposed upon the majority. It relies upon terror and oppression, a controlled press and radio, fixed elections, and the suppression of personal freedoms.

I believe that it must be the policy of the United States to support free peoples who are resisting attempted subjugation by armed minorities or by outside pressures.

I believe that we must assist free peoples to work out their own destinies in their own way.

I believe that our help should be primarily through economic and financial aid which is essential to economic stability and orderly political processes.

The world is not static, and the status quo is not sacred. But we cannot allow changes in the status quo in violation of the charter of the United Nations by such methods as coercion, or by such subterfuges as political infiltration. In helping free and independent nations to maintain their freedom, the United States will be giving effect to the principles of the charter of the United Nations. . . .

It would be an unspeakable tragedy if these countries, which have struggled so long against overwhelming odds, should lose that victory for which they sacrificed so much. Collapse of free institutions and loss of independence would be disastrous not only for them but for the world. Discouragement and possibly failure would quickly be the lot of neighboring peoples striving to maintain their freedom and independence.

• *President Truman delivered this message to Congress on 12 March 1947. It was in response to requests from Turkey and Greece for financial and economic help.*

Secretary of State George C. Marshall proposed the Marshall Plan. It was ambitious and costly. It gave the Western European countries, weakened by war, the money they needed to make their economies prosperous. By doing so, the United States hoped—as Marshall said—to "create social and economic conditions in which free institutions could flourish." The money was also offered to the Soviets, but they refused both to take part and to allow the Eastern European countries they controlled to do so. Some members of Congress objected to the cost—$16 billion. The measure, passed in 1948, achieved its goal: the European economies revived spectacularly, and no Western European country became either communist or pro-Soviet.

THE BERLIN CRISIS. The Soviets reacted to Truman's policy by becoming even more hostile. In 1948, they tried to force the United States and its allies out of Berlin by cutting off access to the city by land. Berlin was surrounded by the Soviet zone of Germany. Truman responded by mounting a massive airlift into the city, in order to keep it supplied. The crisis could have led to war, but the Soviets backed down. It pointed out, however, the need for greater military strength with which to confront the Soviet Government.

A series of executive and legislative actions

during Truman's presidency, notably the National Security Act of 1947, both strengthened and reorganized the armed forces. At Truman's request, Congress increased military spending. A peacetime draft was introduced and the Central Intelligence Agency (CIA) was created. In 1949, the United States signed the North Atlantic Treaty with Canada and 10 Western European countries, creating NATO, an organization of joint defense against the Soviet Union. Additionally, scientists began working on a nuclear weapon more powerful than the atomic bomb in order to outmatch the nuclear weapons that the Soviet Union now possessed. The hydrogen bomb was first detonated in 1952. All these measures signaled the beginning of what American journalist Walter Lippmann called the cold war. That "war" was a political-military confrontation between the United States and the Soviet Union that ended up lasting 45 years. The cold war greatly changed both countries. In the 1940s, however, these actions gained broad approval from the public. The American people began to think of Truman as a tough, reliable defender of American-style freedom around the world.

However, Truman was not popular with the American public. The contrast between himself and Roosevelt worked against him. Franklin Roosevelt had an upper-class New York elegance; Harry Truman's midwestern ways seemed limited and frequently awkward. During the first year of Truman's presidency, the nation went through a lot of painful

UNITED STATES NOTE ON BERLIN BLOCKAGE AND AIRLIFT

The United States Government wishes to call to the attention of the Soviet Government the extremely serious international situation which has been brought about by the actions of the Soviet Government in imposing restrictive measures on transport which amount now to a blockade against the sectors in Berlin occupied by the United States, United Kingdom and France. The United States Government regards these measures of blockade as a clear violation of existing Berlin by the four occupying powers. . . .

In order that there should be no misunderstanding whatsoever on this point, the United States Government categorically asserts that it is in occupation of its sector in Berlin with free access thereto as a matter of established right deriving from the defeat and surrender of Germany and confirmed by formal agreements among the principal Allies. It further declares that it will not be induced by threats, pressures or other actions to abandon these rights. It is hoped that the Soviet Government entertains no doubts whatsoever on this point. . . .

The responsibility which this Government bears for the physical well-being and the safety of the German population in its sector of Berlin is outstandingly humanitarian in character. This population includes hundreds of thousands of women and children, whose health and safety are dependent on the continued use of adequate facilities for moving food, medical supplies and other items indispensable to the maintenance of human life in the western sectors of Berlin. The most elemental of these human rights which both our Governments are solemnly pledged to protect are thus placed in jeopardy by these restrictions. It is intolerable that any one of the occupying authorities should attempt to impose a blockade upon the people of Berlin. . . .

• *The United States delivered this note to the Soviet Government on 6 July 1948, two weeks after the Soviets began their blockade of Berlin.*

adjustments while changing from a wartime to a peacetime economy. Strikes and shortages caused much public unhappiness. In 1946, the Republicans won a decisive victory, capturing both houses of Congress. The President and Congress argued for the next two years, but accomplished little. Although many Americans appreciated Truman's firmness with the Soviets, he seemed to many to be a small man in a big job.

ELECTION OF 1948. As the presidential election of 1948 approached, Truman's prospects seemed dismal. Many Democrats had rejected his leadership. Two even ran against him for presi-

▲ *"Early in May (1948) I had an idea—perhaps the only one that the critics admitted was entirely my own. In order to circumvent the gloom and pessimism being spread by the polls and by false propaganda in the press, I decided that I would go directly to the people in all parts of the country with a personal message from the President. It would mean riding thousands of miles by train and making talks at all hours at stops along the way where crowds could be assembled to hear the facts. But it was the only alternative." Harry S. Truman,* Years of Trial and Hope, Volume Two.

When President Truman's popularity hit an all-time low, he set out on a whistle-stop tour to the West Coast and back. He delivered 76 speeches on this train tour and he was particularly pleased that 71 of them were "off the cuff" using only very brief notes. (National Park Service; photographer: Abbie Rowe, Courtesy Harry S. Truman Library.)

dent. Henry A. Wallace formed the Progressive Party, composed of Democrats who objected to Truman's tough Soviet policy.

At the same time, Southern Democratic leaders organized the States Rights (Dixiecrat) Party. They chose Governor J. Strom Thurmond of South Carolina to run against Truman. They were outraged that Truman had suggested federal laws against lynching. He also suggested laws to end discrimination against African Americans in the armed forces and in interstate transportation. Truman's position on civil rights was complex. He had been brought up to believe that African Americans were inferior. Nevertheless, he felt that they were entitled to fair treatment. He was outraged at Southern whites'

Every Democratic platform since 1932 has stressed the devotion of our party to the constitutional ideal of civil rights. But what aroused many Southerners now was that I meant to put this pledge into practice. When the Southerners saw in 1948 that I meant to put it into effect, they bolted the party. When J. Strom Thurmond, the governor of South Carolina, who headed the revolt, made his dramatic departure from the convention floor in Philadelphia with his followers, he was asked by a reporter to clarify his position.

"President Truman is only following the platform that Roosevelt advocated," the reporter pointed out.

"I agree," Thurmond replied, "but Truman really *means* it."

• *Harry S. Truman,* Years of Trial and Hope, Volume Two.

assaults on African American veterans of the war.

The South, he said, was "80 years behind the times." He was also upset because Soviet propaganda was able to make use of Southern whites' racial prejudice to picture the United States as an evil, prejudiced country.

The Republicans, confident of victory, chose Governor Thomas E. Dewey of New York to run against Truman. The Democrats renominated Truman, who chose Alben W. Barkley of Kentucky as his running mate. Barkley was an old friend from the U.S. Senate. There were four major candidates in the race: Truman, Dewey, Wallace, and Thurmond. Neither of the last two were expected to win, but at least they would take votes away from Truman.

Dewey was confident of victory. He was a serious, formal man who had made his reputation as a crime-busting district attorney. He did not campaign very hard. Truman, however, traveled all over the country by train, speaking often from the back of the last car. He denounced the Republican-controlled Congress and their failure to act on his recommendations. He called them the do-nothing Congress. Nevertheless, all the news media, and the opinion polls, predicted his defeat.

Truman did not give up. On 2 November, he scored perhaps the greatest upset in the history of presidential elections. He defeated Dewey by 303 electoral votes to 189. Thurmond won 39 electoral votes and Wallace won none. Truman's tireless campaigning, matched against Dewey's inactivity, partly explain the victory. Another explanation was that Truman, once a farmer and always a midwesterner, appealed the most to voters in several normally Republican Midwestern states. Truman won their votes by promising higher price supports for farm products.

The voters also elected a Democratic-controlled Congress in 1948. Truman was now in a position to get laws passed that reflected his goals for the coun-

On the morning after the election, President Truman held up a copy of the Chicago Daily Tribune. *The headline states* "DEWEY DEFEATS TRUMAN." (Courtesy Harry S. Truman Library.)

try. His policy was to preserve and extend the Roosevelt social program called the New Deal. The main features of this program were government aid to farmers and retired people and an income-tax system that taxed the rich heavily and legal protection for organized labor. To emphasize the similarity between himself and Roosevelt, Truman called his program the Fair Deal.

Many Republicans claimed that both the New Deal and the Fair Deal involved too much government control. They said that they were too much like communist economic policies. In view of the hostility between the United States and the Soviet Union, they felt that the United States should reject anything that resembled communism. But Truman successfully defended the New Deal pro-

"I cautioned the Congress against being frightened away from health insurance by the scare words "socialized medicine" which some people were bandying about. I wanted no part of socialized medicine, and I knew the American people did not. Under socialized medicine all doctors would work as employees of the government. I was proposing no such system. I reminded the Congress that, although we were a rich nation and could afford many things, we could not afford ill-health. Our belief in insurance against unnecessary loss had become an American tradition, and what was now offered was a workable plan for insurance against loss of one of our most priceless possessions—health."

• *Harry S. Truman,* Years of Trial and Hope, Volume Two.

grams, and even enlarged them. Social Security was expanded to include 10 million more citizens. The Employment Act of 1946 increased the federal role in managing the economy. The National Housing Act of 1949 put the federal government in the businesses of providing low-income housing, and rebuilding central cities.

The wave of costly and bothersome strikes in 1945 and 1946 caused organized labor to become unpopular with many Americans. Truman felt that he could deal with labor disputes just by using his executive powers, but in 1947 the Republican Congress passed the Taft-Hartley Act. This act sharply limited some of the powers that labor unions had acquired during New Deal times. Truman vetoed the act, but Congress overrode his veto and passed it. All throughout his second term, Truman tried in vain to get the Taft-Hartley Act repealed. His other major failure was his inability to persuade Congress that the United States should have national compulsory health insurance, a program which conservatives opposed as "socialized medicine." They felt it was too much like a socialist or communist system.

Truman's presidency also saw basic reforms in U.S. Government. The Twenty-second Amendment, passed by Congress during his second term, limited future presidents to two terms. This guaranteed that no one would duplicate Franklin Roosevelt's 12-year presidency. The Presidential Succession Act of 1947 put the congressional leaders, rather than the cabinet, next in line after the vice president. And, on a somewhat smaller scale, Truman was responsible for repairing and restoring the White House, the structure of which was on the verge of collapse when he moved in.

COMMUNISM AT HOME. The most heated domestic issue of Truman's presidency was the extent of communist influence inside the United States. The debate over this issue grew increasingly loud during his eight years, because of the sudden onset of the cold war, and the Soviets' known habits of spying and overthrowing governments. Many Americans in 1946 and 1947 were concerned that Soviet agents might be active in the United States. They were even afraid that some Americans could be communist spies. Truman and Attorney General Tom Clark shared this concern. In 1947, they set up the "Loyalty Oath" program that tried to identify and eliminate all government employees who might prove to be pro-Soviet. This program uncovered almost no disloyal employees.

At the same time, some prominent Republicans felt (as previously explained) that in fact New Deal Democrats were little better than communists. They believed that there were important Democrats with pro-Soviet sympathies in the government. During 1947 and 1948, when the Republicans controlled Congress, they even used the House Committee on Un-American Activities (HUAC) to investigate alleged communist connections of several people who had been part of Roosevelt's administration. Truman denounced these investigations as politically motivated. But, as the cold war deepened, many Americans came to share the Republicans' feelings.

The Democratic Congress passed acts to restrict immigration (McCarran-Walter Immigration and Nationality Act) and control the opinions and activities of government workers (McCarran Internal Security Act of 1950). Truman vetoed both acts, but Congress overrode his vetoes.

Eventually, some Republicans became violent, reckless, and abusive in their attacks on the administration. Their leader, beginning in 1950, was Senator Joseph R. McCarthy of Wisconsin. Among his charges was the claim that Secretary of State Dean Acheson and Secretary of Defense George C. Marshall favored communism. Truman first ignored McCarthy; he later criticized him. Neither tactic was effective, and the false accusations were still going on when Truman retired from the presidency in 1953.

THE COLD WAR IN ASIA. During Truman's second term, the focus of the cold war suddenly shifted to Asia. Since the end of World War II, China had been in turmoil, with two rival groups—the communists and the nationalists—fighting to

---

TRUMAN'S VETO OF THE INTERNAL SECURITY ACT OF 1950 (THE MCCARRAN ACT)

... There is no more fundamental axiom of American freedom than the familiar statement: In a free country we punish men for the crimes they commit but never for the opinions they have. And the reason this is fundamental to freedom is not, as many suppose, that it protects the few unorthodox from suppression of the majority. To permit freedom of expression is primarily for the benefit of the majority, because it protects criticism, and criticism leads to progress. ...

• *President Truman vetoed The McCarran Act with this message to the U.S. House of Representatives on 22 September 1950. He said that passage of this act would be "the greatest danger to freedom of speech, press and assembly since the alien and sedition laws of 1798." It was named after Senator Patrick A. McCarran of Nevada.*

---

control the country. The United States tried without success to aid the nationalists, but by October 1949, the communists had managed to gain control of all China, except the island of Taiwan, still in nationalist hands. To many Americans, and Republicans in particular, a communist-controlled China represented a major loss in the ongoing struggle with the Soviet Union. Some Republicans blamed Truman's administration, and especially "communist sympathizers" in it, for "losing China."

THE KOREAN WAR. After World War II, Korea was divided into two countries, since the Korean communists could not agree with other parties on unifying the country. North (communist) Korea and South (non-communist) Korea were divided by a border called the thirty-eighth parallel. In June

President Truman flew to Wake Island in the Pacific and met with General Douglas MacArthur on 15 October 1950. Truman wanted to discuss possible intervention by China into the Korean War. MacArthur assured Truman that the war was won and China would not become involved in the war. (U.S. Department of State, Courtesy Harry S. Truman Library.)

ANNOUNCEMENT RELIEVING GENERAL DOUGLAS MACARTHUR

With deep regret, I have concluded that General of the Army Douglas MacArthur is unable to give his whole-hearted support to the policies of the United States Government and of the United Nations in matters pertaining to his official duties. In view of the specific responsibilities imposed upon me by the Constitution of the United States and the added responsibility which has been entrusted to me by the United Nations, I have decided that I must make a change of command in the Far East. I have, therefore, relieved General MacArthur of his commands and have designated Lieutenant General Matthew B. Ridgway as his successor.

Full and vigorous debate on matters of national policy is a vital element in the constitutional system of our free democracy. It is fundamental, however, that military commanders must be governed by the policies and directives issued to them in the manner provided by our laws and Constitution. In time of crisis, the consideration is particularly compelling.

General MacArthur's place in history as one of our greatest commanders is fully established. The Nation owes him a debt of gratitude for the distinguished and exceptional service which he has rendered his country in posts of great responsibility. For that reason I repeat my regret at the necessity for the action I feel compelled to take in his case.

• *President Truman's announcement was handed to reporters at a news conference on 11 April 1951.*

1950, North Korean troops invaded South Korea in large numbers. Truman and his advisers saw the attack as a continuation of Soviet-sponsored aggression in Asia. It was a clear case for the use of the Truman Doctrine.

Fearing war with the Soviet Union, Truman at first limited U.S. aid to air and naval support. But, as North Korean troops were about to overrun South Korea, the United Nations—at the suggestion of the United States—voted to oppose the invasion with armed force, and the United States began sending its own soldiers to fight in Korea.

Truman's aim was to repel North Korean aggression and punish North Korea for its attacks. His military commander in Korea, Douglas MacArthur, was a famous World War II general, able but also arrogant. After two discouraging months, MacArthur, by a surprise invasion at Inchon, managed to drive the North Korean Army out of South Korea. Truman then gave him authority to pursue them into North Korea. This decision brought China into the war, as it feared a U.S. military presence on its border. In the winter of 1950–1951, 300,000 Chinese troops crossed into North Korea, overpowering the U.S. Army and forcing it back into South Korea.

MacArthur then urged Truman to bomb China. Truman believed that this action would make the Soviet Union enter the war, and thus provoke a world conflict. He refused and decided to seek a cease-fire. When MacArthur failed to cooperate with the new policy, Truman removed him from command. A huge storm of public anger followed, but died down gradually as the unrealistic nature of MacArthur's views became obvious.

The cease-fire talks with North Korea began in 1951. They were still in progress when Truman left office in 1953. The war, still causing many U.S. casualties, was continuing on a reduced scale. The mood of the public had changed from enthusiasm to weariness and frustration, as it was to do in the case of Vietnam just 15 years later.

OTHER FOREIGN INITIATIVES. Two of Truman's other foreign-policy contributions not directly related to the cold war deserve mention. The first was his decision in 1948 to recognize the newly created Jewish state of Israel, making the United States the first country to do so. Truman's decision was popular with a large section of the American public, both Jewish and Christian, which supported the idea of a Jewish homeland. On the other hand, by appearing to place the United States on the side of Israel, it alienated the Arab leaders of the Middle East, who thought of the Jewish state as an extension of European colonialism, and set the stage for decades of anti-American feeling in the area.

The other contribution was the Point Four program, the first U.S. effort to provide technical and economic aid to underdeveloped nations.

CORRUPTION. During Truman's second term, news stories revealed that several people he had appointed to federal positions had used their offices illegally, exchanging government favors for money. Two agencies involved were the Reconstruction Finance Corporation and the Bureau of Internal Revenue. Truman's typical reaction was to deny the charges, and often to delay dismissing the officials even after their corruption had been proved. Some were his personal friends, and Truman was loyal to his friends. His defense of these men raised questions about how much more corruption there might be in his administration. This contributed to his unpopularity.

LEAVING OFFICE. Harry S. Truman could have run for a third term in 1952, but he recognized that the issues which Republicans called "the three C's" (although one was a K)—Communism, Corruption, and Korea—had made him too unpopular. He therefore announced his retirement and persuaded the governor of Illinois, Adlai E. Stevenson II (an intellectual politician with a reputation for clean government), to be the next Democratic candidate for president. In the general election, however, Stevenson lost overwhelmingly to the Republican candidate Dwight D. Eisenhower.

LAST YEARS. Truman returned to Independence, Missouri after his presidency. He wrote his memoirs and was active in Democratic politics for

POINT FOUR PROGRAM

. . . The grinding poverty and the lack of economic opportunity for many millions of people in the economically underdeveloped parts of Africa, the Near and Far East, and certain regions of Central and South America, constitute one of the greatest challenges of the world today. In spite of their age-old economic and social handicaps, the peoples in these areas have, in recent decades, been stirred and awakened. The spread of industrial civilization, the growing understanding of modern concepts of government, and the impact of two World Wars have changed their lives and their outlook. They are eager to play a greater part in the community of nations.

All these areas have a common problem. They must create a firm economic base for the democratic aspirations of their citizens. Without such an economic base, they will be unable to meet the expectations which the modern world has aroused in their peoples. If they are frustrated and disappointed, they may turn to false doctrines which hold that the way of progress lies through tyranny. . . .

The aid that is needed falls roughly into two categories. The first is the technical, scientific, and managerial knowledge necessary to economic development. This category includes not only medical and educational knowledge, and assistance and advice in such basic fields as sanitation, communication, road building, and governmental services, but also, and perhaps most important, assistance in the survey of resources and in planning for long-range economic development.

The second category is production goods—machinery and equipment—and financial assistance in the creation of productive enterprises. The underdeveloped areas need capital for port and harbor development, roads and communications, irrigation and drainage projects, as well as for public utilities and the whole range of extractive, processing, and manufacturing industries. Much of the capital required can be provided by these areas themselves, in spite of their low standards of living. But much must come from abroad.

The two categories of aid are closely related. Technical assistance is necessary to lay the ground-work for productive investment. Investment, in turn, brings with it technical assistance. In general, however, technical surveys of resources and of the possibilities of economic development must precede substantial capital investment. Furthermore, in many of the areas concerned, technical assistance in improving sanitation, communications, or education is required to create conditions in which capital investment can be fruitful. . . .

• *In his Inaugural Address, President Truman said: "In the coming years, our program for peace and freedom will emphasize four major courses of action." Six months later, on 24 June 1949, he sent a special message to Congress urging an assistance program for underdeveloped countries.*

In his memoirs, Truman wrote that this was not a lending program or a giveaway program. He estimated that "an improvement of only two percent in the living standards of Asia and Africa would keep the industrial plants of the United States, Great Britain, and France going at full tilt for a century just to keep up with the increased demand for goods and services."

Congress enacted the President's proposal on 5 June 1950.

another 10 years. In the 1960s, as the cold war continued, Truman's reputation began to rise. He was seen as an honest, plain-speaking leader. More important, however, was the view of him as a commander in chief who had helped save many countries from Soviet domination, and who had strengthened United States military power. He died in Kansas City Hospital on 26 December 1972.

VICE PRESIDENT

Alben William Barkley
(1877–1956)

CHRONOLOGICAL EVENTS

1877	Born, Lowes, Kentucky, 24 November
1897	Graduated from Marvin College, Clinton, Kentucky
1904	Elected prosecuting attorney, McCracken County, Kentucky
1912	Elected to U.S. House of Representatives
1926	Elected to U.S. Senate
1937	Elected Senate majority leader
1948	Elected vice president
1954	Again elected to U.S. Senate
1956	Died, Lexington, Virginia, 30 April

BIOGRAPHY

Born on a tobacco farm in western Kentucky, he began life as Willie Alben Barkley, but later reversed the order to make his name sound more formal. After working his way through college as a janitor, he briefly attended the University of Virginia Law School. In 1904, Barkley campaigned on horseback for prosecuting attorney, and later served as county judge. Winning a seat in the U.S. House of Representatives in 1912, he strongly supported Woodrow Wilson's progressive programs. A noted orator and an enthusiastic campaigner, Barkley defeated an incumbent Republican to win election to the U.S. Senate.

During the early years of the New Deal, Barkley worked as chief lieutenant to the Democratic majority leader, Joseph Robinson. When Robinson died in 1937, Barkley ran for the leadership against the popular Mississippi Senator Pat Harrison. President Franklin D. Roosevelt's intervention helped Barkley achieve a one-vote victory. Thereafter senators perceived him as Roosevelt's spokesman in the Senate, rather than as the Democratic leader. In 1944, Roosevelt vetoed a revenue bill against Barkley's recommendation. Furious, Barkley resigned as majority leader, but Democratic senators unanimously reelected him. From then on, Barkley spoke more for the senators than for the President.

That act of rebellion cost Barkley the vice presidential nomination in 1944. It went to Harry S. Truman, who became president when Roosevelt died. Yet Barkley supported President Truman wholeheartedly in the Senate. At the Democratic convention in 1948, Barkley delivered a rousing keynote address and was nominated to run with Truman. Their unexpected victory shifted him from floor leader of the Senate to presiding officer. Barkley became the last vice president to spend most of his time presiding over the Senate. As vice president, he enjoyed the President's full confidence and support. A 70-year-old widower, the Vice President also won headlines by courting and marrying an attractive young widow. People affectionately called him "Old Alben" and the "Veep."

Although Barkley tried for the Democratic nomination for president in 1952, his advanced age worked against him. Going back to Kentucky, he won another term in the Senate. While addressing students at Washington and Lee University in 1956, he collapsed and died on the stage.

THE CABINET

SECRETARY OF STATE
Edward R. Stettinius, Jr., 1945
James F. Byrnes, 1945
George C. Marshall, 1947
Dean G. Acheson, 1949

SECRETARY OF WAR[1]
Henry L. Stimson, 1945
Robert P. Patterson, 1945
Kenneth C. Royall, 1947

SECRETARY OF THE TREASURY
Henry Morgenthau, Jr., 1945
Fred M. Vinson, 1945
John W. Snyder, 1946, 1949

POSTMASTER GENERAL
Frank C. Walker, 1945
Robert E. Hannegan, 1945
Jesse M. Donaldson, 1947, 1949

ATTORNEY GENERAL
Francis Biddle, 1945
Thomas C. Clark, 1945, 1949
J. Howard McGrath, 1949
James P. McGranery, 1952

SECRETARY OF THE NAVY[1]
James V. Forrestal, 1945

Henry L. Stimson is shown here with his wife, Mabel, in July 1945. (Courtesy Herbert Hoover Presidential Library-Museum.)

Henry L. Stimson (1867–1950). Stimson served in the cabinets of four presidents. He was secretary of war under William Howard Taft (1911–1913); secretary of state under Herbert Hoover (1929–1933); and secretary of war under Franklin D. Roosevelt and Harry S. Truman (1940–1945).

Stimson advised Presidents Roosevelt and Truman on nuclear fission, heading the committee that decided on the use of the atomic bomb to end the war with Japan. He also proposed that the United States share its nuclear knowledge with the Soviet Union and bring nuclear fission and its development under international controls.

THE CABINET

SECRETARY OF THE INTERIOR
Harold L. Ickes, 1945
Julius A. Krug, 1946, 1949
Oscar L. Chapman, 1949, 1950

SECRETARY OF AGRICULTURE
Claude R. Wickard, 1945
Clinton P. Anderson, 1945
Charles F. Brannan, 1948

SECRETARY OF COMMERCE
Henry A. Wallace, 1945
W. Averell Harriman, 1947
Charles Sawyer, 1948, 1949

SECRETARY OF LABOR
Frances Perkins, 1945
Lewis B. Schwellenbach, 1945
Maurice J. Tobin, 1948, 1949

SECRETARY OF DEFENSE[1]
James V. Forrestal, 1947
Louis A. Johnson, 1949
George C. Marshall, 1950
Robert A. Lovett, 1951

1. Department of Defense established 26 July 1947 incorporating the Departments of War, the Navy, the Army, and the Air Force.

George C. Marshall (left) is shown being sworn in by Chief Justice Fred M. Vinson. (Courtesy National Archives.)

George C. Marshall (1880–1959). Marshall was appointed secretary of state by President Harry S. Truman in 1947. He had previously served as U.S. Army Chief of Staff (1939–1945) in the administration of Franklin D. Roosevelt and was the principal Allied strategist in World War II.

As secretary of state, Marshall proposed an economic recovery plan to revive the European economy, which Truman named the Marshall Plan (1947). In 1953, Marshall received the Nobel Peace Prize for the success of his plan.

From 1950 to 1951, Marshall served as secretary of defense. He was responsible for rebuilding the U.S. armed forces and for the military defense planning in Korea.

Harry S. Truman taking the oath of office after the death of President Franklin D. Roosevelt. 12 April 1945. From left to right: Secretary of Labor Frances Perkins; Secretary of War Henry Stimson; Secretary of Commerce Henry Wallace; War Production Board Administrator Julius Krug; Secretary of the Navy James Forrestal; Secretary of Agriculture Claude Wickard; War Manpower Commissioner Francis McNamee; Attorney General Francis Biddle; Harry S. Truman; Secretary of State Edward Stettinius; Bess Truman; Chief Justice Harlan Stone; Speaker of the House Sam Rayburn; Fred Vinson, Office of War Mobilization and Reconversion; House Minority Leader Joseph Martin; Representative Robert Rampseck; and House Majority Leader John McCormack. (Courtesy Harry S. Truman Library.)

FAMILY

CHRONOLOGICAL EVENTS

13 February 1885	Elizabeth (Bess) Virginia Wallace born
28 June 1919	Bess Wallace married Harry S. Truman
17 February 1924	Daughter, Mary Margaret, born
26 December 1972	Harry S. Truman died
18 October 1982	Bess Truman died

Bess Wallace met Harry S. Truman, when they were in the fifth grade. They lived only two and one-half blocks away from each other.

(Courtesy Library of Congress.)

45

▲ *President Truman on vacation with Bess and their daughter, Margaret. She graduated from George Washington University in 1946, one year after her father became president. She pursued a singing career for awhile. When a critic at the Washington Post gave her a bad review, the President threatened to punch him in the nose.*

In 1956, she married Clifton Daniel, Jr., a journalist for The New York Times. *She has written* Harry S. Truman *and* Bess, *biographies of her parents. She has also written several mysteries which take place in Washington.*
(U.S. Navy, Courtesy Harry S. Truman Library.)

▲ *Former President Truman with his four grandchildren in March 1968. This was his last trip to Key West, Florida.* (Courtesy Harry S. Truman Library.)

PLACES

HARRY S. TRUMAN BIRTHPLACE STATE HISTORIC SITE

1109 Truman Avenue • Lamar, Missouri 64759 • Tel: (417) 682-2279

Located two miles east of U.S. 71, one block off Highway 160, approximately 32 miles northeast of Joplin. Open daily Monday to Saturday from 10 A.M. to 4 P.M.; Sundays, 1 May to 1 November, from 12 P.M. to 6 P.M.; Sundays, 1 November to 1 May, from 12 P.M. to 5 P.M. Closed Thanksgiving, Christmas, New Year's Day, and Easter. No admission fee. Operated and maintained by the Division of Parks and Recreation, State of Missouri.

President Truman's father, John, purchased the birthplace property for $685 in 1882. The bedroom where the future president was born measures only 6 feet, 6 inches by 10 feet, 9 inches. (Courtesy Harry S. Truman Library.)

President Truman's father, John, purchased the birthplace property in 1880 and built a six-room, white frame house on it between 1880 and 1882. It did not have electricity, running water, or a bathroom. In 1884, Harry S. Truman was born in the downstairs southwest bedroom. When he was 10 months old, the Truman family sold the property and moved to Harrisonville, Missouri. The home then had a succession of private owners for a period of 72 years.

In 1957, the birthplace property was purchased by the United Automobile Workers of America and given to the State of Missouri. Between 1957 and 1959, the home was both restored and furnished with furniture common to the period of President Truman's birth. It was not possible to place original furnishings in the birthplace home because the Truman family had not owned the home or lived in the area for over seven decades. Truman's parents were also deceased at the time of its restoration. The last time President Truman visited the site was 19 April 1959, when it was dedicated and officially opened to the public.

HARRY S. TRUMAN NATIONAL HISTORIC SITE

219 North Delaware Site • P.O. Box 4139 • Independence, Missouri 64050 • Tel: (816) 254-2720

Located 12 miles east of Kansas City. Can be reached by Interstate 70 (Exit 12) or Interstate 435 (Exit 60). Tickets must be purchased from the Truman Home Ticket and Information Center. Open daily from 8:30 A.M. to 5 P.M. Closed Thanksgiving, Christmas, and New Year's Day. Tours are not available on Mondays between Labor Day and Memorial Day. Tours of the neighborhood are available during the summer months. Parking is limited. Operated and maintained by the National Park Service, Department of the Interior.

During Truman's presidency, the North Delaware Street home became known as the Summer White House. When Truman left office he and his wife returned to Independence, Missouri, and lived out the rest of their days there. (Courtesy National Park Service, Harry S. Truman National Historic Site)

The Truman home was built by George Porterfield Gates, the maternal grandfather of President Truman's wife, Bess Wallace, in 1867. In 1904, following the death of her father, the Wallace family moved into the two-and-a-half-story, white frame house. Six years later, the courtship of Harry and Bess began. Upon their marriage in June 1919, the Gates–Wallace house became their home and remained so for more than half a century.

Mrs. Truman donated the site to the United States Government in her will. In 1982, Secretary of the Interior James G. Watt declared the property a National Historic Site to be administered by the National Park Service. On 23 May 1983, President Ronald Reagan signed Public Law 98-32, authorizing the Harry S. Truman National Historic Site.

HARRY S. TRUMAN LIBRARY

U.S. Highway 24 and Delaware Street • Independence, Missouri 64050 • Tel: (816) 833-1225

Located 10 miles east of Kansas City. The museum is open daily from 9 A.M. to 5 P.M. Closed Thanksgiving, Christmas, and New Year's Day. Admission fee, with discounts available for students in organized tour groups. Arrangements must be made in advance. Handicapped accessible. Educational and research facilities are open by appointment only. Administered by the National Archives and Records Administration.

The library was designed by local architect Alonzo H. Gentry, with the assistance of Edward Neild. From 1957 to 1966, Harry S. Truman often walked the mile from his home to the library where he had his office. (Courtesy Harry S. Truman Library.) ▶

The library houses approximately 14 million pages of manuscript material (5 million of which are White House files), 40,000 books, and more than 1,400 microfilm copies of printed material. It also contains an audiovisual collection consisting of approximately 90,000 still photographs, 500 hours of disc and tape recordings, more than 400 motion pictures and 75 hours of videotape recordings. The museum contains approximately 30,000 objects, including gifts from foreign heads of state, personal items, and other mementos. It was dedicated on 6 July 1957.

◀ *The graves of President and Mrs. Truman are located in the library courtyard.* (Courtesy Harry S. Truman Library.)

Dwight D. Eisenhower

CHRONOLOGICAL EVENTS

14 October 1890	Born, Denison, Texas
12 June 1915	Graduated from U.S. Military Academy, West Point, New York
1922	Assigned to Panama Canal Zone
1925–1926	Attended Command and General Staff School, Fort Leavenworth, Kansas
1928–1929	Attended Army War College, Washington, D.C.
1932	Joined the staff of General Douglas MacArthur
1935	Assigned to the Philippines
27 March 1942	Promoted to major general
11 June 1942	Appointed commander of U.S. forces in Europe
7 July 1942	Promoted to lieutenant general; directed the invasion of North Africa
11 February 1943	Promoted to general; directed the invasions of Sicily and Italy
24 December 1943	Appointed Supreme Allied Commander, Allied Expeditionary Forces
6 June 1944	Directed the invasion of Normandy, D-Day
December 1944	Promoted to five-star general
7 May 1945	Accepted surrender of German army, Rheims, France
1945–1948	Served as U.S. Army chief of staff
24 June 1947	Accepted appointment as president of Columbia University, New York, assumed duties 12 October 1948
19 December 1950	Appointed Supreme Allied Commander, Europe by foreign ministers of NATO
4 November 1952	Elected president
20 January 1953	Inaugurated president
8 December 1953	Delivered Atoms for Peace address at United Nations
6 November 1956	Reelected president
21 January 1957	Inaugurated president
9 March 1957	Announced Eisenhower Doctrine; proposed nuclear test ban
24 September 1957	Dispatched federal troops to Little Rock, Arkansas to ensure enrollment of African American students into the local high school
25 November 1957	Suffered a severe stroke
25 September 1959	Met with Soviet Premier Nikita Khrushchev at Camp David
1961	Retired to his farm in Gettysburg, Pennsylvania
14 October 1965	Published first volume of memoirs, *Mandate for Change*
20 April 1966	Published second volume of memoirs, *Waging Peace*
28 March 1969	Died, Washington, D.C.

BIOGRAPHY

Dwight David ("Ike") Eisenhower was born on 14 October 1890 in Denison, Texas, the third of six sons of Ida and David Eisenhower. The family moved to Abilene, Kansas the next year. In 1911, Eisenhower entered the U.S. Military Academy at West Point, New York. When he graduated in 1915, he was 125th in conduct and 61st in academics of 164 cadets. Known as "the class the stars fell on," the class of 1915 produced 59 generals. Two graduates, Eisenhower and Omar Bradley, won five stars—General of the Army.

Eisenhower met Mamie Doud at his first assignment at Fort Sam Houston, San Antonio, Texas. They married in 1916. Their first son, Dwight David ("Icky"), died of scarlet fever at the age of three. Their second son, John, was born in 1922.

From 1922 to 1924, Major Eisenhower was assigned to the Panama Canal Zone. He attended the Command and General Staff School at Fort Leavenworth, Kansas from 1925 to 1926 and graduated first out of 275 officers. He attended the Army War College in 1928–1929 and was assigned to Washington in 1929 in the office of assistant secretary of war. In the early 1930s, Eisenhower joined the staff of General Douglas MacArthur, who was then army chief of staff. In 1932, he helped MacArthur deal with the Bonus Marchers, the 15,000 veterans of World War I who had come to Washington to demand the money that had been awarded to them. In 1935, he accompanied MacArthur to the Philippines, returning to the United States in 1939 as war began in Europe.

Dwight David Eisenhower married Mamie Geneva Doud at her parents' home in Denver, Colorado on 1 July 1916. (Courtesy Dwight D. Eisenhower Library.)

WORLD WAR II. In 1941, Eisenhower won a brigadier general's star and received national attention for his performance in the Louisiana war games, a large training exercise. When the Japanese attacked Pearl Harbor in 1941 and the United States officially entered World War II, Army Chief of Staff George C. Marshall summoned Eisenhower to Washington as assistant chief of staff to write war plans. Several months later he was promoted to major general. In July 1942, he received his third star as lieutenant general, and he later commanded the Allied invasions of North Africa, Sicily, and Italy. In December 1943, President Franklin D. Roosevelt named him Supreme Allied Commander, Allied Expeditionary Force (SHAEF). Eisenhower's staff prepared OVERLORD, his plan for invading Europe. On 6 June 1944, as his son, John, was graduating from West Point, Operation OVERLORD began. Allied troops crossed the English Channel on D-Day in the largest fleet of ships ever assembled and landed on the Normandy beaches as 23,000 paratroopers dropped onto the French countryside behind the German Atlantic defenses. Early the following winter, Eisenhower was promoted to General of the Army. In May 1945, 11 months after D-Day, Germany surrendered. In August 1945, U.S. planes dropped atomic bombs on Hiroshima and Nagasaki; Japan surrendered soon after. Eisenhower replaced Marshall as army chief of staff in November 1945.

In 1948, Eisenhower retired from the army and became president of Columbia University in New York. His book about the war, *Crusade in Europe*, became a best-seller. Eisenhower's wartime popularity had made him a presidential contender as early as 1943. He subsequently turned down the offers of both parties to run for president.

In 1950, the World War II Atlantic allies formed the North Atlantic Treaty Organization (NATO) as protection against Soviet aggression. Eisenhower

President Franklin D. Roosevelt appointed Eisenhower Supreme Allied Commander, Allied Expeditionary Forces, in December 1943. That same month they visited an airfield in Sicily. (U.S. Army, Courtesy Dwight D. Eisenhower Library.)

Portrait of Eisenhower when he was U.S. Army chief of staff (November 1947). Although this cheerful portrait of Eisenhower was well-received by the American public, one of his biographers said that Eisenhower did not particularly like it. (Courtesy Dwight D. Eisenhower Library.)

Eisenhower visited with paratroopers from the 101st Airborne Division the evening before D-Day. (Courtesy Dwight D. Eisenhower Library.)

left Columbia in December 1950. One month later, President Harry S. Truman appointed him the first Supreme Allied Commander, Europe (SACEUR), for NATO.

FIRST TERM AS PRESIDENT. Eisenhower resigned from NATO in May 1952 and from the army soon after receiving the Republican nomination for president. He defeated Senator Robert A. Taft of Ohio on the first ballot at the Republican National Convention. Richard M. Nixon, a young (age 39) senator from California, was chosen as his running mate.

Eisenhower and Nixon campaigned against Truman's policies, criticizing the President's actions in Korea, making charges regarding the presence of communists in the U.S. Government, and claiming corruption in the Truman administration. Most of the rough work was left to Nixon. The

Democratic candidate, Adlai E. Stevenson, governor of Illinois, appeared on television as a likable but weak candidate. Eisenhower's grandfatherly image and his broad grin appealed to voters more than Stevenson's intelligence and wit. Shortly before the election, Eisenhower promised that he would go to Korea to end the war still raging there since 1950. Eisenhower received 55 percent of the popular vote—nearly 34 million votes to Stevenson's 27 million. He received 442 votes to Stevenson's 89 in the Electoral College.

In December 1952, Eisenhower kept his word and went to Korea. Nixon and many other Republicans, including Secretary of State designate John Foster Dulles, wanted to widen the war. They even considered invading China, but Eisenhower knew that that would cause many casualties. An armistice was finally signed at Panmunjom, Korea on 27 July 1953. Korea was left divided into two countries along the 38th parallel.

Although Republicans controlled Congress after the elections in 1952, Eisenhower's agenda was often slowed down by Old Guard conservative Republicans. Senior Republicans believed that Democratic presidents—Franklin D. Roosevelt and Harry S. Truman—had obtained too much authority from Congress during the preceding 20 years. Eisenhower enjoyed great respect for his wartime and postwar service, including his decisive victory over Stevenson in the election, but the Old Guard wanted presidential power cut. Congress wanted to regain greater influence on national policy.

Before the inauguration, John Bricker, a very conservative senator from Ohio, had sponsored an amendment to the Constitution requiring legislative approval of any presidential agreement with another country. A majority of senators from both parties supported "the Bricker amendment" and they were joined by conservative political and professional organizations. The Bricker amendment would have handicapped a president's ability to conduct foreign policy. Eisenhower and his supporters in Congress worked busily through 1954 and managed to switch enough Senate votes to prevent the Bricker amendment from passing.

Eisenhower was a fiscal conservative. He believed that excessive government endangered the U.S. economy as high expenses fed inflation and boosted living costs for all Americans. In addition, wasteful and intrusive programs required higher taxes to pay for them.

Eisenhower cut enough government spending so that the federal government showed a surplus. Paying fewer taxes by 1955, Americans spent more on new purchases in the biggest economic boom since World War II. Early in his first term, Eisenhower also struggled with the conservative Republicans' demand for reduced military spending. The President hoped to avoid excessive defense cutbacks, but the recent end to the Korean War gave

Eisenhower defeated Robert Taft on the first ballot at the Republican national convention, July 1952. (Courtesy Dwight D. Eisenhower Library.)

ATOMS FOR PEACE

. . . To hasten the day when fear of the atom will begin to disappear from the minds of people, and the governments of the East and West, there are certain steps that can be taken now. . . .

I would be prepared to submit to the Congress of the United States, and with every expectation of approval, any such plan that would:

First — encourage world-wide investigation into the most effective peacetime uses of fissionable material, and with the certainty that they had all the material needed for the conduct of all experiments that were appropriate;

Second — begin to diminish the potential destructive power of the world's atomic stockpiles;

Third — allow all peoples of all nations to see that, in this enlightened age, the great powers of the earth, both of the East and of the West, are interested in human aspirations first, rather than in building up the armaments of war;

Fourth — open up a new channel for peaceful discussion, and initiate at least a new approach to the many difficult problems that must be solved in both private and public conversations, if the world is to shake off the inertia imposed by fear, and is to make positive progress toward peace.

Against the dark background of the atomic bomb, the United States does not wish merely to present strength, but also the desire and the hope for peace. . . .

• *The Soviet Union had built a hydrogen bomb by the summer of 1953. A nuclear war involving the entire world was becoming more likely. President Eisenhower spoke to the United Nations General Assembly on 8 December 1953 in order to propose that the United States and the Soviet Union work together on the peaceful use of nuclear power.*

"Eisenhower made the most effective use of it (his military experience) in late October, when he uttered the most memorable sound bite of the campaign: 'I shall go to Korea.' The statement underscored the fact that in one corner stood the leader of the greatest military effort in American history, in the other, a man with no real military experience. Stevenson had no credible response; he and his advisers had already decided that a similar response from him would not be taken seriously." Alonzo L. Hamby, "1952," in Running for President: The Candidates and Their Images, *edited by Arthur M. Schlesinger, Jr. Eisenhower went to Korea, as he had promised, in December 1952.* (U.S. Army, Courtesy Dwight D. Eisenhower Library.)

the conservatives an effective argument in favor of reduced spending. Eisenhower reorganized the Defense Department in 1953 and in 1958 and created a "new look" military. He favored having fewer soldiers in uniform and a greater dependency on nuclear weapons for defense. Nuclear arms cost less than large numbers of armed troops. Yet Eisenhower admitted impatience with constant requests for newer weapons. He discussed this in

his Farewell Address (see p. 65).

In 1952, before he became a presidential candidate, Eisenhower had resisted John Foster Dulles's idea that the United States should meet Soviet aggression with "massive retaliation" (the use of nuclear weapons rather than conventional forces). Eisenhower believed that U.S. military strength by itself was enough to deter Soviet aggression. By 1954, Eisenhower had become bolder, promising quick "massive retaliation" in return for any Soviet attack on the United States. He wanted to avoid another surprise attack like Pearl Harbor, especially in the atomic age.

McCARTHYISM. When the Republicans took control of Congress in 1952, Joseph McCarthy, a Wisconsin senator and World War II Marine veteran, won the chairmanship of the Permanent Committee on Investigations of the Senate Committee on Government Operations. Undertaking a hunt for communists in the government, he started with the State Department. He received early support from other politicians and from the public. His information looked accurate although in most cases it turned out not to be, and he fed the public fear of communism. McCarthy investigated many Americans, destroying their reputations, careers, families and, sometimes, their lives. He blamed State Department experts for China's fall to communism and some were fired. Many people including college professors, newspaper and television reporters, and entertainers were ruined by "McCarthyism." This reckless persecution was carried out under the protection of congressional immunity. McCarthy frequently made baseless charges and damaged the integrity of the U.S. political and judicial systems. McCarthy did not pose a real threat to Eisenhower but his tactics and allies insulted Eisenhower's personal beliefs and hopes for the future of the Republican Party. When McCarthy attacked the U.S. Army, Eisenhower began to work behind the scenes against him. In the 1954 Army-McCarthy hearings, a lawyer for the army challenged McCarthy while television viewers watched and, in the end, this helped bring McCarthy down. The Democrats regained congressional control in 1954 elections. McCarthy lost his chairmanship, and he was censured by the Senate in December 1954.

VIETNAM. Vietnamese nationalists, (Viet Minh), led by Ho Chi Minh, hoped for U.S. support for independence when Japan was defeated, but it never came. France returned to Indochina after World War II to recover a colony in chaos, but the Viet Minh under Ho Chi Minh continued a jungle war. From 1949 on, the United States aided the French with money and weapons, but France was losing and the French people tired quickly of another war.

By 1954, the Viet Minh had surrounded three key French bases at Dien Bien Phu in northeast Vietnam. France asked the United States for more help—aircraft, troops, and U.S. bomber missions—to save Dien Bien Phu. Eisenhower was torn between his commitment to contain communism and his desire to avoid involving U.S. forces in another war like Korea. In the end, he refused to send troops and Dien Bien Phu fell to the communists in May 1954. France lost a war and, in the Geneva Convention that followed, a colony. The Viet Minh, under Ho Chi Minh, continued to fight against the new South Vietnamese government established at Geneva which enjoyed increasing U.S. aid. Some claim that Eisenhower kept the United States out of war in Vietnam by refusing to send troops to fight against the Vietnamese nationalists. Actually he involved the country in Indochina by providing U.S. advisers and financial support.

In mid-July 1955, Eisenhower flew to Geneva for a summit meeting with the new Soviet leaders who had come to power after Joseph Stalin's death. Both sides agreed that nuclear war presented too many horrors, and the number of nuclear threats made by the United States and the Soviet Union in the "cold war" slowly lessened after the summit. The next year brought a lower level of confrontation than that which had previously characterized the cold war.

Eisenhower was vacationing in Colorado in September 1955 when he had a heart attack. He spent a month in a military hospital in Denver and returned to work by his 65th birthday. In February 1956, he announced his candidacy for reelection, seeing no possible successor with enough experience. When his campaign began in June, he became ill again, this time with ileitis, a digestive problem requiring surgery. Supporters and opponents alike wondered if he was well enough to live out a second term.

International politics changed quickly in 1956. President Gamal Abdel Nasser of Egypt ordered his army to seize the Suez Canal, connecting the Mediterranean Sea and the Red Sea. The canal, although in Egypt, was held by the British. Without informing the United States, France and Israel allied with Great Britain to attack Suez and recapture the canal. This old-fashioned colonialism shocked Eisenhower. He urged the United Nations to pass resolutions threatening economic sanctions against Great Britain, France, and Israel if they did not change their plans. The old allies from World War II felt betrayed, but Eisenhower's stand gained him popularity with undeveloped countries.

The same year, Hungary tried to free itself from Soviet domination. Soviet armies quickly invaded Hungary with tanks to put down the uprising, killing 40,000 people. Hungarian leaders begged for help from the United States, but Eisenhower felt that Hungary was too close to the Soviet Union and too isolated from NATO Europe for him to order U.S. forces into action. He also refused to drop supplies and weapons by parachute. A total of 150,000 Hungarians escaped to Austria and Eisenhower allowed 21,000 to immigrate to the United States

Eisenhower defeated Adlai E. Stevenson again in November 1956 by a greater margin than in 1952. He received 35.5 million votes to Stevenson's 26 million, and 457 electoral votes to Stevenson's 73.

EISENHOWER'S SECOND TERM. Eisenhower had appointed Earl Warren, the former governor of California, to the Supreme Court in 1954. Warren led the Court to a series of decisions on civil rights and civil liberties. One of the most important of these cases was *Brown v. Board of Education*, which ordered the desegregation of public schools, finding that "separate but equal"

President Eisenhower discussed civil rights issues with African American leaders in June 1958. From left to right: Martin Luther King, Jr.; F. Frederick Morrow; Eisenhower; A. Philip Randolph; and Attorney General William P. Rogers. Rogers established the Civil Rights Division of the Department of Justice, and he advised the President about his decision to enforce desegregation in Little Rock. (National Park Service, Courtesy Dwight D. Eisenhower Library.)

THE SITUATION IN LITTLE ROCK

. . . This morning the mob again gathered in front of the Central High School of Little Rock, obviously for the purpose of again preventing the carrying out of the Court's order relating to the admission of Negro children to that school.

Whenever normal agencies prove inadequate to the task and it becomes necessary for the executive branch of the federal government to use its powers and authority to uphold federal courts, the president's responsibility is inescapable.

In accordance with that responsibility, I have today issued an Executive Order directing the use of troops under federal authority to aid in the execution of federal law at Little Rock, Arkansas. This became necessary when my proclamation of yesterday was not observed, and the obstruction of justice still continues.

It is important that the reasons for my action be understood by all our citizens.

As you know, the Supreme Court of the United States has decided that separate public educational facilities for the races are inherently unequal and therefore compulsory school segregation laws are unconstitutional.

Our personal opinions about the decision have no bearing on the matter of enforcement; the responsibility and authority of the Supreme Court to interpret the Constitution are very clear. Local federal courts were instructed by the Supreme Court to issue such orders and decrees as might be necessary to achieve admission to public schools without regard to race—and with all deliberate speed. . . .

Proper and sensible observance of the law then demanded the respectful obedience which the nation has a right to expect from all its people. This, unfortunately, has not been the case at Little Rock. Certain misguided persons, many of them imported into Little Rock by agitators, have insisted upon defying the law and have sought to bring it into disrepute. The orders of the court have thus been frustrated.

The very basis of our individual rights and freedoms rests upon the certainty that the president and the executive branch of government will support and insure the carrying out of the decisions of the federal courts, even, when necessary with all the means at the president's command.

Unless the president did so, anarchy would result.

There would be no security for any except that which each one of us could provide for himself.

The interest of the nation in the proper fulfillment of the law's requirements cannot yield to opposition and demonstrations by some few persons.

Mob rule cannot be allowed to override the decisions of our courts. . . .

• *In September 1957, President Eisenhower returned from vacation when the white mobs in Little Rock became violent and the mayor of that city asked for federal protection. Eisenhower spoke from the White House and pointed out that he was not pushing integration but rather defending the rule of law.*

education was unconstitutional. In September 1957, Governor Orval Faubus of Arkansas called out the National Guard to keep African Americans out of the all-white Central High School in Little Rock. Eisenhower acted quickly and decisively, sending the 101st Airborne Division to Little Rock to enforce the law.

The Civil Rights Act of 1960, the first civil rights bill in 80 years, was primarily concerned with voting rights. Eisenhower supported its guarantee of

President Eisenhower signed the proclamation admitting Hawaii into the Union as the 50th state on 21 August 1959. Hawaii had been annexed in 1898 during the administration of William McKinley.

Eisenhower is shown here with Vice President Richard M. Nixon (seated, left) and Speaker of the House Sam Rayburn (seated, right). Standing, left to right, Lorrin Thurston, chairman of the Hawaiian Statehood Commission; Edward Johnston, former secretary of the treasury of Hawaii; Secretary of the Interior Frederick A. Seaton; Senator-elect Oren E. Long; and Representative-elect Daniel K. Inouye. (Courtesy Dwight D. Eisenhower.)

voting rights to southern African Americans who were refused routinely when they attempted to register to vote. The law gave some power to the federal government to enforce civil rights.

SPUTNIK. The United States and Soviets began "the race for space" on 4 October 1957, when the Soviet Union launched Sputnik I, a satellite that circled the earth. A month later a larger Sputnik II carried a dog into space to simulate human space flight. The United States feared that the Soviet Union had superior technology. Americans worried that these achievements meant that the Soviets could shoot their ballistic missiles longer distances than the United States could shoot its missiles. This would make it easier for the Soviets to attack without fear of a counterattack. Democrats claimed that Eisenhower had created a

"missile gap." Without changing his beliefs in government economies, Eisenhower ordered an accelerated U.S. space program, paid for in part by defense economies in other areas. He also requested Congress to increase federal aid to education.

PROBLEMS IN TWO HEMISPHERES. An arms race accelerated in the Middle East by spring 1958. The Egyptian president, Gamal Abdel Nasser, sought other Islamic nations to join his United Arab Republic (UAR), almost igniting revolutions against the ruling monarchies in Jordan, Iraq, and Saudi Arabia. Eisenhower feared that if Nasser unified all Arab states, he would share with them the weapons and aid that he received from the Soviets, and cut the flow of oil to the West. In Lebanon, Christian and Islamic soldiers attacked each other, and Muslims rioted against Christian president Canille Chamoun after he awarded himself a second term, violating the national constitution. A worried Chamoun asked for U.S. military help after Nasser encouraged a coup in Iraq, killing the royal family.

Eisenhower responded with his first military operation as president. On 15 July 1958, U.S. Marines landed in Lebanon with the goal of restoring stability in the area. By late October, they had completed their mission and left. Eisenhower had shown his critics that he was capable of using U.S. troops in military actions, not limiting himself to nuclear weapons.

Another crisis flared up in August when the Chinese Nationalists on Formosa (Taiwan), survivors of the 1948 revolution that left the Chinese Communists in charge of the mainland, increased their troops to 100,000 on Quemoy and Matsu, two small islands off the Chinese mainland. Communist artillery from the mainland bombarded the islands. Eisenhower sent two more aircraft carriers to the Seventh Fleet in the Formosa Straits. When the firing continued, Eisenhower and his aides considered the use of nuclear weapons. The President said publicly that he opposed "appeasement" of the communists but there would be no war. Communist Chinese and U.S. diplomats met and the communists agreed to reduce artillery attacks to odd-numbered days only so that the Nationalists could resupply their troops on even-numbered days. Soon the Nationalist island forces were reduced slightly, and the crisis lessened.

At the end of November 1958, the Soviet leader Nikita Khrushchev issued an ultimatum to Great Britain, France, and the United States demanding that they leave their occupation zones in Berlin within six months. Led by Eisenhower, the occupying powers stood firm. When he visited the President at Camp David, Maryland, in September 1959, Khrushchev acknowledged that he had backed down on the Berlin deadline. He also shocked Eisenhower by advocating total elimination of nuclear and other weapons in a speech at

the United Nations. The Soviet leader generally criticized the United States while enjoying Eisenhower's hospitality. Responding to the Soviet premier's Berlin concessions, Eisenhower agreed to a Paris summit conference the following May.

On 1 January 1959, Fulgencio Batista, the longtime Cuban dictator, fled Havana. Fidel Castro, the leader of the revolutionary forces, entered Havana to take power. Within two weeks, Castro legalized communism in Cuba. By month's end, he continued killing Batista supporters and making anti-U.S. statements. It began a pattern of Cuban-U.S. antagonisms that continued late in the century.

U-2 INCIDENT. The U.S.-Soviet summit was scheduled for Paris in mid-May 1960, and

Premier Nikita Khrushchev canceled the invitation for President Eisenhower to visit the Soviet Union after the Soviet Union shot down a U-2 spy plane.
(Courtesy Dwight D. Eisenhower Library.)

Eisenhower planned to close a deal with Khrushchev on nuclear testing that would live as the supreme accomplishment of his administration. He planned to continue to Moscow afterward. On 1 May, he was told that a U.S. U-2 high-altitude reconnaissance plane had been reported missing leaving from an airbase in Turkey on a mission to photograph Soviet bases. Khrushchev announced that the Soviet Union had downed a U.S. spy plane over Soviet airspace. Believing that the pilot was dead and that the Soviets lacked proof, Eisenhower denied that the plane was on a spy mission and said that the pilot was doing weather research when trouble with his oxygen supply led him off course. The Soviet premier had trapped Eisenhower. He announced that the Soviets had recovered parts of the plane and captured the pilot, Francis Gary Powers. He provided the film Powers had shot as evidence of aerial spying. A week later, Eisenhower and Khrushchev met in Paris for the summit. Khrushchev heaped his anger on the United States and canceled his invitation for Eisenhower to visit the Soviet Union. Hopes for an agreement on nuclear testing crashed like the plane. The French president, Charles DeGaulle, the host of the summit who had been increasingly skeptical of NATO, was offended by Khrushchev's performance. As a result, relations between France and the rest of the Atlantic alliance improved.

RETIREMENT. Richard M. Nixon, the Republican presidential candidate in 1960, narrowly lost the election to Senator John F. Kennedy of Massachusetts. Eisenhower genuinely preferred Nixon to Kennedy, but he was slow to endorse him. The outgoing President predicted a gloomy future in his farewell speech on 17 January 1961. Eisenhower warned of a military too entwined with weapons builders, creating a "military-industrial complex," a phrase that became part of the English language.

In 1966, long after he left the White House, Eisenhower listed 23 accomplishments of his presidency: Hawaii and Alaska were admitted as states; the completed St. Lawrence Seaway enabled ships to carry cargo year round from the Great Lakes to the Atlantic Ocean without waiting for spring icemelts; no American died in combat during his administration after the Korean War ended; taxes were cut more than any time before; the first civil rights law in 80 years was passed; communism was stopped in Iran, Guatemala, Lebanon, Formosa, and South Vietnam; the Defense Department was reorganized; the law authorizing the interstate highway system was passed; inflation was reduced; a space program was begun; a powerful ballistic missile system was built; the Polaris missile system was deployed at sea; the Kerr-Mills bill provided medical care for senior citizens; desegregation of D.C. and the military; there were eight years of fiscal and financial responsibility; federal survivors insurance was extended to 10 million needy people; aid to education

President Eisenhower greeted President-elect John F. Kennedy at the White House on 6 December 1960. They met to prepare for a smooth transition. (National Park Service, Courtesy Dwight D. Eisenhower Library.)

EISENHOWER'S FAREWELL ADDRESS

Until the latest of our world conflicts, the United States had no armaments industry. American makers of plowshares could, with time and as required, make swords as well. But now we can no longer risk emergency improvisation of national defense; we have been compelled to create a permanent armaments industry of vast proportions. Added to this, three and a half million men and women are directly engaged in the defense establishment. We annually spend on military security more than the net income of all United States corporations.

This conjunction of an immense military establishment and a large arms industry is new in the American experience. The total influence—economic, political, even spiritual—is felt in every city, every statehouse, every office of the federal government. We recognize the imperative need for this development. Yet we must not fail to comprehend its grave implications. Our toil, resources, and livelihood are all involved; so is the very structure of our society.

In the councils of government, we must guard against the acquisition of unwarranted influence, whether sought or unsought, by the military-industrial complex. The potential for the disastrous rise of misplaced power exists and will persist.

We must never let the weight of this combination endanger our liberties or democratic processes. We should take nothing for granted. Only an alert and knowledgeable citizenry can compel the proper meshing of the huge industrial and military machinery of defense with our peaceful methods and goals, so that security and liberty may prosper together. . . .

- *President Eisenhower spoke to the nation for the last time on the evening of 17 January 1961. The warning about a military-industrial complex was particularly notable coming from an old soldier.*

was continued; military dismantlement after wartime was prevented for the first time; federal court orders on desegregation were enforced by federal action in Little Rock; more than 20 friendly visits to other nations around the world were made; the Department of Health, Education, and Welfare was established; Congress approved social progress plans for Latin America; and the Atoms for Peace proposal, a program to divert nuclear research from destructive to peaceful purposes, was approved. After listing these achievements, Eisenhower added: "I had dashed these off the top of my head."

After John F. Kennedy's inauguration in January 1961, Eisenhower and his wife returned to Gettysburg, Pennsylvania, where they had bought a farm in 1950. In November 1963, *Mandate for Change*, the first of Eisenhower's two White House memoirs, was published. In 1965, *Waging Peace*, the second volume, was released. Neither book enjoyed the success of *Crusade in Europe. At Ease : Stories I Tell My Friends* was published in 1967. This collection of anecdotes had greater success than the two memoirs.

Eisenhower had several more heart attacks, in 1965 and 1968. He watched the wedding of his grandson, David, to Nixon's daughter, Julie, on television from a hospital bed. On 28 March 1969, Dwight Eisenhower looked at his son, John, and said, "I want to go; God take me." He had "come from the heart of America," he had told Great Britain in a famous speech in 1945, and now Eisenhower was buried there, back in Abilene, on 2 April 1969.

VICE PRESIDENT

Richard Milhous Nixon
(1913–1994)

CHRONOLOGICAL EVENTS

1913	Born, Yorba Linda, California, 9 January
1934	Graduated from Whittier College, California
1942	Enlisted in the U.S. Navy
1946	Elected to U.S. House of Representatives
1950	Elected to U.S. Senate
1952	Elected vice president
1960	Ran unsuccessfully for president
1968	Elected president
1974	Resigned as president
1994	Died, New York, New York, 22 April

BIOGRAPHY

Richard M. Nixon described his life as a series of crises. Born into a Quaker family in Yorba Linda, California, he worked in his father's grocery store. Graduating from Whittier College and Duke Law School, Nixon abandoned Quaker pacifism to serve in the navy during World War II.

After the war, some Southern California busi-

nessmen recruited Nixon to run for Congress. He beat the incumbent Democrat by questioning his loyalty. As a member of the House Committee on Un-American Activities, Nixon seized national attention by siding with Whittaker Chambers, the witness who accused the former State Department official Alger Hiss of being a communist.

Nixon ran for the U.S. Senate in 1950 against the Democratic Representative Helen Gahagan Douglas, whom he accused of being a "pink lady." She tagged him "Tricky Dick." After only two years in the Senate, the 39-year-old Nixon was chosen to run for vice president with the popular General Dwight D. Eisenhower. "Ike" employed Nixon to make highly partisan attacks on Democrats regarding corruption, communism, and the war in Korea. But Nixon himself was accused of accepting a secret fund from wealthy businessmen. Going on television to defend himself, Nixon's "Checkers" speech (named for the dog he had received as a present) saved his candidacy.

Becoming vice president, Nixon overhauled the office. He was the first vice president to move to the Executive Office Building next to the White House, rather than spend most of his time at the Capitol. He campaigned widely for Republican candidates and lobbied for the President's programs in Congress. When Eisenhower suffered a heart attack in 1955, Nixon presided at cabinet meetings and kept the government operating smoothly.

Yet Eisenhower remained uncertain about Nixon and tried to persuade him to take a cabinet post rather than run for reelection. Nixon refused and stayed on the ticket. During one of his numerous diplomatic visits overseas, Nixon and his wife Pat withstood an attack by a Venezuelan mob. In Moscow, he conducted a "kitchen debate" with Soviet Premier Nikita Khrushchev.

Nixon ran as the Republican candidate for president in 1960 but lost narrowly to Massachusetts Senator John F. Kennedy. Defeated next for governor of California, he seemed finished in politics. Then in 1968 he reemerged as a "New Nixon" and won the presidency.

THE
CABINET

SECRETARY OF STATE
John Foster Dulles, 1953, 1957
Christian A. Herter, 1959

SECRETARY OF THE TREASURY
George M. Humphrey, 1953, 1957
Robert B. Anderson, 1957

POSTMASTER GENERAL
Arthur E. Summerfield, 1953, 1957

ATTORNEY GENERAL
Herbert Brownell, Jr., 1953
William P. Rogers, 1958

SECRETARY OF THE INTERIOR
Douglas McKay, 1953
Frederick A. Seaton, 1956, 1957

SECRETARY OF AGRICULTURE
Ezra Taft Benson, 1953, 1957

SECRETARY OF COMMERCE
Sinclair Weeks, 1953, 1957
Lewis L. Strauss, 1958
Frederick H. Mueller, 1959

SECRETARY OF LABOR
Martin P. Durkin, 1953
James P. Mitchell, 1953, 1957

SECRETARY OF DEFENSE
Charles E. Wilson, 1953, 1957
Neil H. McElroy, 1957
Thomas S. Gates, Jr., 1959

SECRETARY OF HEALTH, EDUCATION, AND WELFARE[1]
Oveta Culp Hobby, 1953
Marion B. Fulson, 1955, 1957
Arthur S. Flemming, 1958

1. Department of Health, Education, and Welfare established 1 April 1953.

(Courtesy Dwight D. Eisenhower Library.)

John Foster Dulles (1888–1959). Dulles was appointed secretary of state by President Dwight D. Eisenhower in 1953. He had previously served in the U.S. Senate. In 1950, he had been the chief architect of the peace treaty with Japan.

As secretary of state, between 1953 and 1959, Dulles was the major force in U.S. foreign policy, personally traveling over 500,000 miles. He planned the Southeast Asia Treaty Organization (SEATO) in 1954, and the Central Treaty Organization (CENTO) in 1959, as attempts to combat communism by forming mutual defense alliances.

In January 1954, Dulles announced that the United States would use the deterrent of "massive retaliation" (the use of nuclear weapons rather than conventional forces) to defend itself and its allies against the spread of communism.

Dulles resigned early in 1959. He died of cancer later that year.

President Eisenhower with cabinet members and others. 8 May 1953. Clockwise from the lower left, Henry Cabot Lodge, Jr., chief U.S. representative to the United Nations; Secretary of the Interior Douglas McKay; Secretary of the Treasury George M. Humphrey; Vice President Richard M. Nixon; Attorney General Herbert Brownell, Jr.; Secretary of Commerce Sinclair Weeks; Secretary of Health, Education, and Welfare Oveta Culp Hobby; Presidential Assistant Sherman Adams; Budget Director Joseph M. Dodge; Acting Director of Defense Mobilization Arthur S. Flemming; Secretary of Labor Martin P. Durkin; Postmaster General Arthur E. Summerfield; Secretary of State John Foster Dulles; President Eisenhower; Secretary of Defense Charles E. Wilson; Secretary of Agriculture Ezra Taft Benson; and Director of Mutual Security Harold E. Stassen. Standing in the rear are Philip Young (left), chairman of the Civil Service Commission and Robert Cutler, assistant to the President for National Security Affairs. (Courtesy Dwight D. Eisenhower Library.)

FAMILY

CHRONOLOGICAL EVENTS

14 November 1896	Marie (Mamie) Geneva Doud born	3 August 1922	Son, John Sheldon Doud, born
1 July 1916	Mamie Doud married Dwight D. Eisenhower	28 March 1969	Dwight D. Eisenhower died
		11 November 1979	Mamie Eisenhower died

(Courtesy Library of Congress.)

Mamie Doud met Dwight D. Eisenhower, when she was 18 years old. She had just finished her education, and he had been assigned to Fort Sam Houston, San Antonio, Texas. Less than one year later, they were married in her parents' home in Denver, Colorado. They moved to the Panama Canal Zone in 1922. She was to live in more than 30 places throughout the world before his election to the presidency. They did not have a permanent home until they retired to Gettysburg, Pennsylvania, in January 1961.

▲ *Their first son, Doud Dwight (Icky) Eisenhower, was born in 1917 but died of scarlet fever in 1921. Their second son, John, graduated from the United States Military Academy at West Point on D-Day, June 1944. He was a major, serving in Korea, when his father was elected president. He married Barbara Jean Thompson in 1947 at Fort Monroe, Virginia. He retired from the army in 1963, and he has written a number of history books.* (Courtesy Library of Congress.)

The Eisenhowers had four grandchildren. Two of them, Dwight David II and Barbara Anne, were in the reviewing stand at Eisenhower's first Inauguration. David is looking at Vice President Richard M. Nixon's younger daughter, Julie. They were married 15 years later.

David has written several books, including Eisenhower at War : 1943–1945, *a biography of his grandfather. Julie has also written several books, including* Pat Nixon: The Untold Story, *a biography of her mother.*

(Courtesy Dwight D. Eisenhower Library.) ▶

PLACES

EISENHOWER BIRTHPLACE STATE HISTORIC SITE

208 East Day Street
Denison, Texas 75020
Tel: (903) 465-8908

*Dwight D. Eisenhower
was born in a two-story
house built around
1880 in Denison, Texas.
It has been restored to
its 1890 appearance.*
(Courtesy Dwight D. Eisenhower
Birthplace State Historic Site.)

*Located in Grayson County, approximately 10 miles north of Sherman. Can be reached via U.S. 69 and U.S.
75. Open daily from 9 A.M. to 5 P.M. Closed Thanksgiving, Christmas, and New Year's Day. Admission fee.
Children ages 5 and under admitted free. Tours available. Handicapped accessible. Administered by the Texas
Parks and Wildlife Department.*

Dwight D. Eisenhower was born in a two-story white house on the corner of Lamar and Day streets in Denison, Texas on 14 October 1890. In March 1892, when he was two years old, his family moved to Abilene, Kansas. The birthplace was virtually forgotten until Eisenhower was elected president in 1952. Before his election, rumors had started to circulate that he was born in Denison. Even Eisenhower himself was unaware of that fact since he listed Tyler, Texas as his birthplace when he was a cadet at West Point.

Fred Conn, publisher of the *Herald,* the Denison newspaper, had checked an 1891 city directory and found a listing for the Eisenhower family. Conn then confirmed the birthplace house with Eisenhower's mother, Ida, and in 1953, the Eisenhower Birthplace Foundation, Inc. was chartered to begin the restoration. Five years later, the property was deeded to the Texas State Parks Board (now the Texas Parks and Wildlife Department), and plans were drawn for the state historic site.

The site, encompassing approximately 10 acres, features historic buildings, railroad trails, picnic sites, and hiking paths. A visitor center contains a video resource room, a bookstore, and a gift shop.

THE EISENHOWER CENTER

Abilene, Kansas 67410 • Tel: (913) 263-4751

Since the boyhood home of President Eisenhower was opened to the public on 22 June 1947, more than 2 million people have visited the site. All the furnishings belonged to the Eisenhower family.
(Courtesy Dwight D. Eisenhower Library.)

Located two miles south of the Abilene exit, off Interstate 70, on Kansas Highway 15. All buildings at the center are open daily from 9 A.M. to 4:45 P.M. Closed Thanksgiving, Christmas, and New Year's Day. During the summer, beginning on Memorial Day, both the museum and the visitor center are open until 5:45 P.M. Admission fee charged for the exhibit area of the museum. Children ages 15 and under admitted free. No fee is charged at the other buildings. The research facilities of the library are open Monday through Friday from 9 A.M. to 4:45 P.M. No admission fee charged, but advance written application must be made to the Director. Handicapped accessible. The center contains the Dwight D. Eisenhower Library, the Eisenhower Boyhood Home, the museum, the visitor center, and the Place of Meditation (burial site). Administered by the National Archives and Records Administration.

In 1892, Eisenhower's grandfather, Jacob, purchased the boyhood home and three acres of land from the J. M. Fisher bankruptcy trustee. Two years later, he deeded the property to his son Abraham. In 1898, Abraham entered the ministry and sold the property to Eisenhower's parents, David and Ida. Shortly after Eisenhower's family moved in, a one-story section was added to the east side, and in 1915, a new kitchen and a pantry were added to the north side.

The boyhood home, built in 1887 by Ephraim Ellis, a schoolteacher, is a two-story frame house. It was occupied by members of the Eisenhower family from 1898 until the death of Eisenhower's mother, Ida, in 1946. Upon her death, the property was deeded to the Eisenhower Foundation by her sons, under the stipulation that the home should always remain—as much as possible—exactly as it was when the family lived in it. It was opened to the public on 22 June 1947.

The library is located across from the museum. It contains the papers, books, and other historical materials relating to Eisenhower's presidency and prior military career. It was designed primarily as a research institution and contains a research room, archival stacks, offices for the staff, a photographic laboratory, and an auditorium. The library was dedicated on 1 May 1962.

The museum, designed by Wilton Beckett of Los Angeles, is located just east of the boyhood home. It contains five major galleries that exhibit photographs and items associated with President Eisenhower, his wife Mamie, and other members of the Eisenhower family. In 1971, an addition was completed which doubled the exhibit space of the original building. It was dedicated on Veterans Day 1954.

At the groundbreaking ceremony for the library on 13 October 1959, President Eisenhower stated: "When this library is filled with documents, and scholars come here to probe into some of the facts of the past half century, I hope that they, as we today, are concerned primarily with the ideas, principles, and trends that provide guides to a free, rich, peaceful future in which all peoples can achieve ever-rising levels of human well-being." (Courtesy Dwight D. Eisenhower Library.) ▶

EISENHOWER NATIONAL HISTORIC SITE

P.O. Box 1080 • Gettysburg, Pennsylvania 17325-1080 • Tel: (717) 334-1124

The Eisenhower Tour Center is located one-half mile south of the town center of Gettysburg on State Route 123. Visitors are not permitted to travel directly to the site; shuttle buses leave the parking area regularly. Open daily, 1 April through 31 October, Wednesday to Sunday, from 8:30 A.M. to 4 P.M. Closed Thanksgiving, Christmas, and New Year's Day. Admission fee. Children ages 5 and under admitted free. Handicapped accessible. The site contains the farmhouse, a barn, the guest house, and a reception center. Administered by the National Park Service, U.S. Department of the Interior.

In 1950, Dwight D. Eisenhower and his wife, Mamie, purchased a 189-acre farm in Gettysburg, Pennsylvania, owned by Allen Reddington. When the remodeling of the farmhouse began, the architects discovered that beneath the brick exterior was a rapidly deteriorating, 200-year-old log cabin frame. A two-story brick section and the kitchen fireplace with a bake oven were salvaged. A new house was built around those features. By March 1955, the new farmhouse was completed under the supervision of chief architect Milton Osborne. It contains eight bedrooms, eight bathrooms, a stately living room, a formal dining room, a large kitchen, an attic studio, and a porch.

For 15 years the Eisenhowers maintained a successful farm that produced corn, wheat, and hay, with a dairy herd and prizewinning purebred Angus cattle. In 1967, they made a gift of their house and property to the U.S. Government, with the agreement they would reside there for life.

Two years later, Eisenhower died at age 78, and his wife lived there until her death in 1978.

▲ *The Gettysburg Farm became known as the Temporary White House when President Eisenhower was recuperating from his first heart attack. Visitors to the farm included Prime Minister Winston Churchill of Great Britain, Premier Nikita Khrushchev of the Soviet Union, and Prime Minister Jawaharlal Nehru of India.* (Courtesy Dwight D. Eisenhower Library.)

John F. Kennedy

35TH PRESIDENT
OF THE UNITED STATES OF AMERICA

CHRONOLOGICAL EVENTS

29 May 1917	Born, Brookline, Massachusetts
20 June 1940	Graduated from Harvard University, Cambridge, Massachusetts
1940	Published *Why England Slept*
1941	Enlisted in U.S. Navy; commissioned as ensign
April 1943	Assumed command of the PT 109; rank of lieutenant
April 1945	Discharged from U.S. Navy
5 November 1946	Elected to U.S. House of Representatives; served three terms
4 November 1952	Elected to U.S. Senate
1 January 1956	Published *Profiles in Courage*
1957	Awarded Pulitzer Prize for *Profiles in Courage*
4 November 1958	Reelected to U.S. Senate
8 November 1960	Elected president
20 January 1961	Inaugurated president
March 1961	Peace Corps established
17–20 April 1961	Bay of Pigs Invasion
August 1961	Berlin Wall built by the Soviet Government
October 1962	Cuban Missile Crisis
23–24 June 1963	Visited West Germany; delivered "Ich bin ein Berliner" speech
25 July 1963	Nuclear Test-Ban Treaty signed
30 August 1963	"Hot line" between Moscow and Washington installed
22 November 1963	Shot by Lee Harvey Oswald; died, Dallas, Texas

BIOGRAPHY

What much of the public remembers best of John Fitzgerald Kennedy's short political life is the Kennedy style: crisp in speech, politically active, alive to the intellectual wing of the Democratic Party. It is truer of Kennedy than of most political figures that understanding his place in history requires an understanding of the way he presented himself to the public. The vigorous Kennedy, in fact, suffered a lifetime of illness. However, in the manner of Franklin Delano Roosevelt, he overcame these disadvantages and transformed them into

assets that indicated personal triumph and bravery.

EARLY YEARS. The development of Kennedy's personality in childhood, was deeply influenced by his father, Joseph Patrick Kennedy. The elder Kennedy was a wealthy and competitive businessman, a New Dealer, and an acquaintance of Franklin D. Roosevelt. He was one of many Americans with money who have wished to pass into the more elegant ranks of society. Although he was of a prominent family himself, he felt the sting of being Irish and Catholic among the Boston

Anglo-American society. His wife, Rose, the daughter of Boston Mayor John F. "Honey-Fitz" Fitzgerald, was also Irish and Catholic. She had been raised as a lady and had a reserved strength to complement the more aggressive personality of her husband.

John F. Kennedy, born on 29 May 1917, was raised in a peculiar mixture of aggressiveness and gentility, like his older brother, Joseph, and his two younger brothers, Robert and Edward. This atmosphere came from their father's business instincts and his social ambitions. The Kennedy parents did not expect their daughters to enter a man's world of achievement, but they were raised to be knowledgeable of the world and sensitive to it. The sons were expected to toughen their minds for its own merits as well as for competitive and social advantages. The sons were sent to private preparatory schools. At home they were put to exercises involving mastery of political thought and knowledge of current news. At the family's summer home in Hyannis Port, on Cape Cod, Massachusetts, the sons learned to sail. Just before World War II, Joseph Kennedy was made ambassador to Great Britain, putting him in the highest levels of the Anglo-American establishment.

These youthful experiences and his rivalry with a competitive older brother, Joe Jr., could have made John—often called Jack—Kennedy driven and very outgoing. But he also had experiences of another sort during his boyhood. He was afflicted with a number of illnesses—a bad back, asthma, and throat swellings. He overcame these illnesses as best as he could, even briefly playing junior varsity football for Harvard. His childhood reading of biographies and historical novels, along with his struggles with sickness, gave Kennedy respect for the virtues of courage and maintaining composure. These were elements of the later Kennedy style.

At Harvard John F. Kennedy worked on his senior thesis about Great Britain's prewar failure to face up fully to the Nazi menace. He was fortunate enough to be able to visit England where he was able to call on his father's staff for help. The thesis was published in 1940 under the title *Why England*

Slept. Ambassador Kennedy made clear his hope for some agreement between the democracies and Nazi Germany. He became an embarrassment to the Roosevelt administration because of his anti-semitism and because he was opposed to supporting Great Britain. He soon resigned his post.

After the entrance of the United States into the war, Joseph Kennedy used his influence to see to it that JFK got a navy commission and then a combat post. He was put in charge of a PT boat, a small trim, fast vessel for which his previous experience in boating had helped to prepare him. While on patrol early in August 1943, as commander of PT 109, he became a hero. He towed a wounded crewman to shore after a Japanese destroyer sliced the craft in half. He then swam a great distance to find help for his men.

When Joe Jr., a navy flier stationed in Great Britain, was killed in a daring mission across the

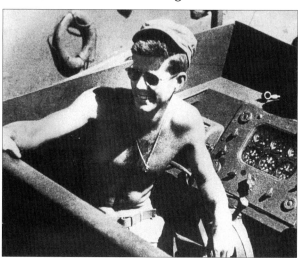

The Japanese destroyer AMAGIRI rammed and sank PT 109, commanded by John Fitzgerald Kennedy, on 2 August 1943 in the Solomon Islands in the Pacific. Kennedy spent 30 of the next 36 hours in the water. He dragged one of his crew three miles by holding the strap of the man's life preserver in his teeth. (Courtesy John F. Kennedy Library and Museum.)

English Channel, JFK became the oldest son. Both tradition and the wishes of a grieving father dictated that he carry on the family's plans and ambitions. In 1946, he ran for the U.S. House of Representatives in a Boston working-class district.

With the help of Kennedy money and a reprint of a magazine story detailing his wartime heroism, Kennedy won the House seat that he would hold until 1953.

U.S. HOUSE OF REPRESENTATIVES. If any one designation best fit the young congressman, it would be that of moderate Democrat. This son of a successful businessman, this upper-class Irish Catholic spokesman for a blue-collar urban district, had no reason to be an impassioned liberal. He denounced foreign aid and expressed approval of the Taft-Hartley Act, which aimed at curbing the power of labor unions. In rightist vocabulary he complained of "do-gooders" and spoke of Roosevelt's sellout to Moscow at the 1945 Yalta Conference. Kennedy also blamed President Harry S. Truman for the loss of China to the communists. He did, however, support more liberal measures such as a minimum wage and a limited national health program.

Well before 1952 Joe Sr. was preparing his son to run for the U.S. Senate seat occupied by the blue-blooded Republican Henry Cabot Lodge Jr. (later to be President Kennedy's ambassador to South Vietnam). Preparation included donating money to charities serving particular ethnic groups, widely circulating the PT 109 article, and high visibility of family members at public events. The Kennedy organization pursued voters with phone calls and the friendly Boston *Post* labeled Lodge a socialist New Dealer. In the 1952 election, the son of the Irish family defeated the offspring of the old Yankee aristocracy.

U.S. SENATE. The uneven pattern of Kennedy's votes and speeches during his years in the Senate marked a move toward the liberal wing of his party. His earlier talk about Yalta and China might have suggested that he would become a politician who saw communists in every government corridor. He might have aligned himself with Wisconsin's Republican rabble-rouser Senator Joseph McCarthy. McCarthy was a family acquaintance, and Robert Kennedy was a counsel on his investigation committee for a short time. But Kennedy distanced himself from McCarthy. During the Senate vote in 1954 on whether to censure McCarthy, Kennedy was undergoing operations for severe back problems. He did not vote one way or the other.

In the Senate, Kennedy voted for some civil rights legislation, but he also supported an amendment to one piece of legislation that would provide jury trials for anyone accused of violating the new law. This would put the enforcement of civil rights at the discretion of white southern juries, an action that some thought would make a mockery of civil rights. In his Senate years, Kennedy expressed a view of the world more complex than he had acknowledged while in the House of Representatives. He supported foreign aid and came around to the liberal view that the communist world was not a single indivisible bloc. His final break from McCarthyism was symbolized in his vote in 1959 to end the requirement that graduate students sign a loyalty pledge as a condition for receiving government loans.

The Senate seat kindled the Kennedy family's ambition for the presidency. At the 1956 Democratic Convention, he narrowly lost a bid to be the running mate of the party's presidential nominee, Adlai Stevenson. Earlier, however, he had made perhaps a different, more significant effort to reach beyond Massachusetts. Like other politicians seeking to widen their reputations, he wrote a book. *Profiles in Courage* bears his name and contains enough of his own work to reflect his perspective. Kennedy made or approved an interesting choice for its theme. The courage discussed in the volume is not the physical courage on which Kennedy the naval hero had made much of his reputation. Rather, it is the political courage displayed by senators in making risky or unpopular decisions. It may be debated whether Kennedy had displayed that more introspective kind of courage up to that time; he later admitted indirectly that he had been less than straightforward on McCarthy. However, his endless struggles with illness—he almost lost his life with Addison's disease—could have developed

Kennedy went to the 1956 Democratic Convention in Chicago hoping to become Adlai Stevenson's running mate, but he lost to Senator Estes Kefauver of Tennessee. Four years later, Kennedy (left) joined Stevenson (center), and Senator Lyndon B. Johnson (right) in a sign of unity at a Democratic Party dinner in Beverly Hills, California, shortly before the Democratic National Convention. (Courtesy National Archives.)

in him a knowledge of private, interior courage. The topic, at any rate, suggests the politician, notably reserved in manner, whose temperament had been formed during his boyhood years of sickness and reading.

By the end of Dwight D. Eisenhower's presidency, the Democratic Party was defining itself as the advocate of a more activist national foreign and domestic policy and, indeed, of a more energetic national mood. The Eisenhower administration, Democrats inaccurately complained, had allowed the country's weapons technology to fall dangerously behind in the face of the Soviet menace. Education from grade school on, so liberals warned, was lacking in difficulty. They championed an alliance, supported by the federal government, between the nation's schools and the technological and scientific community. They argued that this would make the nation both more competitive against the communist nations and tougher and more creative in its domestic life. What could have been more appropriate to the

Democratic liberal cause than a candidate who in naval combat had shown both heroism and technical skill, a Harvard graduate, and a politician whose public image combined a manner of self-possession with a look of energy and intelligence?

ELECTION OF 1960. During the 1960 primaries, the future relations between Kennedy and the liberals could not have been predicted. Senator Hubert Humphrey of Minnesota, the loyal inheritor of the New Deal legacy, was a more believable liberal candidate than the young senator, who had won reelection in 1958 by a wider popular margin than any other senator. Kennedy, moreover, had an immediate obstacle to face. Many believed that prejudice against his Roman Catholic faith might make him a weak contender in the primaries and the general election. In the primary election in overwhelmingly Protestant West Virginia, Kennedy convinced the voters that his religion would not affect his conduct of the presidency. He enjoyed the support of Franklin D. Roosevelt Jr., a living reminder of a president held deep in the affections of the people of this once Depression-ridden state. FDR, Jr. emphasized his candidate's war record and his opponent's lack of one. Kennedy's victory over Humphrey in West Virginia gave him momentum in his successful drive for the Democratic nomination. In the fall campaign against the Republican nominee, Vice President Richard M. Nixon, Kennedy discussed his religion openly and frankly, assuring voters that his faith would not be a problem.

In a time not of widespread suffering but of discontent with a sluggish economy and a frustrating cold war, Kennedy presented himself in 1960 as the candidate of change and growth. This fitted the liberal temper of the moment. In a series of television debates with Vice President Nixon, Kennedy appeared strong and confident against an opponent to whom TV cameras were not flattering. In the South, he gained from the more populist campaigning of his vice presidential partner, Senator Lyndon B. Johnson of Texas. Kennedy's religion may have hurt him slightly in the total popular vote, in which he edged ahead of

ACCEPTANCE SPEECH

. . . I am fully aware of the fact that the Democratic Party, by nominating someone of my faith, has taken on what many regard as a new and hazardous risk—new, at least, since 1928. But I look at it this way: the Democratic Party has once again placed its confidence in the American people, and in their ability to render a free, fair judgment. And you have, at the same time, placed your confidence in me, and in my ability to render a free, fair judgment—to uphold the Constitution and my oath of office—and to reject any kind of religious pressure or obligation that might directly or indirectly interfere with my conduct of the presidency in the national interest. My record of fourteen years supporting public education—supporting complete separation of church and state—and resisting pressure from any source on any issue should be clear by now to everyone.

I hope that no American, considering the really critical issues facing this country, will waste his franchise by voting either for me or against me solely on account of my religious affiliation. It is not relevant, I want to stress, what some other political or religious leader may have said on this subject. It is not relevant what abuses may have existed in other countries or in other times. It is not relevant what pressures, if any, might conceivably be brought to bear on me. I am telling you now what you are entitled to know: that my decisions on every public policy will be my own—as an American, a Democrat and a free man. . . .

For I stand tonight facing West on what was once the last frontier. From the lands that stretch three thousand miles behind me, the pioneers of old gave up their safety, their comfort and sometimes their lives to build a new world here in the West. They were not the captives of their own doubts, the prisoners of their own price tags. Their motto was not "every man for himself"—but "all for the common cause." They were determined to make that new world strong and free, to overcome its hazards and its hardships, to conquer the enemies that threatened from without and within.

Today some would say that those struggles are all over—that all the horizons have been explored—that all the battles have been won—that there is no longer an American frontier.

But I trust that no one in this vast assemblage will agree with those sentiments. For the problems are not all solved and the battles are not all won—and we stand today on the edge of a New Frontier—the frontier of the 1960s—a frontier of unknown opportunities and perils—a frontier of unfulfilled hopes and threats.

Woodrow Wilson's New Freedom promised our nation a new political and economic framework. Franklin Roosevelt's New Deal promised security and succor to those in need. But the New Frontier of which I speak is not a set of promises—it is a set of challenges. It sums up not what I intend to offer the American people, but what I intend to ask of them. It appeals to their pride, not their pocketbook—it holds out the promise of more sacrifice instead of more security. . . .

• *John F. Kennedy addressed the question of his religion in his acceptance speech at the Democratic National Convention in Los Angeles, California on 15 July 1960. The reference to the 1928 risk was the nomination of Alfred E. Smith, governor of New York. Smith was a Catholic. Kennedy first used the famous phrase "the new frontier" in this speech. His advisors became known as "the New Frontiersmen."*

Nixon, but it apparently helped him in some important industrial states; and he won an Electoral College majority. It can be neither proved nor disproved that his wins in Illinois and Texas, necessary to his national victory, profited from vote manipulation by Democratic Party chieftains.

The inaugural address, written by Kennedy's adviser Theodore Sorensen, set the outward tone of Kennedy's administration. It dedicated the country to high standards and demanding goals, although the President appeared committed to no particular ideology. Kennedy's appointees were impressively intelligent and academic. He chose the southern liberal scholar Dean Rusk for secretary of state and, for secretary of defense, he chose the efficient liberal Republican Robert McNamara, who had taught at the Harvard Business School. He selected as one of his advisers the brilliant historian Arthur M. Schlesinger, Jr. In gathering about himself intellectuals and experts, Kennedy seems to have been acting to his own taste. This went with his confidence in trained expertise. For attorney general the President appointed his brother Robert. It was less a policy he was after than an assemblage of ideas and skills, which went with the liberal confidence in trained expertise. Most

CIVIL RIGHTS AND NATIONAL MORALITY

. . . This nation was founded by men of many nations and backgrounds. It was founded on the principle that all men are created equal and that the rights of every man are diminished when the rights of one man are threatened.

Today we are committed to a worldwide struggle to promote and protect the rights of all who wish to be free, and when Americans are sent to Vietnam or West Berlin, we do not ask for whites only. It ought to be possible, therefore, for American students of any color to attend any public institution they select without having to be backed up by troops.

It ought to be possible for American consumers of any color to receive equal service in places of public accommodation, such as hotels and restaurants and theaters and retail stores, without being forced to resort to demonstrations in the street; and it ought to be possible for American citizens of any color to register and to vote in a free election without interference or fear of reprisal.

It ought to be possible, in short, for every American to enjoy the privileges of being American without regard to his race or his color. In short, every American ought to have the right to be treated as he would wish to be treated, as one would wish his children to be treated. But this is not the case. . . .

Next week I shall ask the Congress of the United States to act, to make a commitment it has not fully made in this century to the proposition that race has no place in American life or law. The federal judiciary has upheld that proposition in a series of forthright cases. The executive branch has adopted that proposition in the conduct of its affairs, including the employment of federal personnel, the use of federal facilities, and the sale of federally financed housing.

But there are other necessary measures which only the Congress can provide, and they must be provided at this session. . . .

• *When Governor George Wallace of Alabama promised to "stand in the schoolhouse door" to keep two African Americans from being admitted to the all-white University of Alabama, President Kennedy decided to take immediate action. On the evening of 11 June, he delivered a speech on civil rights on national television. The legislation that Kennedy spoke of was passed by Congress soon after his assassination.*

INAUGURAL ADDRESS

. . . Let the word go forth from this time and place, to friend and foe alike, that the torch has been passed to a new generation of Americans—born in this century, tempered by war, disciplined by a hard and bitter peace, proud of our ancient heritage—and unwilling to witness or permit the slow undoing of those human rights to which this nation has always been committed, and to which we are committed today at home and around the world.

Let every nation know, whether it wishes us well or ill, that we shall pay any price, bear any burden, meet any hardship, support any friend, oppose any foe, in order to assure the survival and the success of liberty.

This much we pledge—and more.

To those old allies whose cultural and spiritual origins we share, we pledge the loyalty of faithful friends. United, there is little we cannot do in a host of cooperative ventures. Divided, there is little we can do—for we dare not meet a powerful challenge at odds and split asunder.

To those new states whom we welcome to the ranks of the free, we pledge our words that one form of colonial control shall not have passed away merely to be replaced by a far greater iron tyranny. We shall not always expect to find them supporting our view. But we shall always hope to find them strongly supporting their own freedom—and to remember that, in the past, those who foolishly sought power by riding the back of the tiger ended up inside.

To those peoples in the huts and villages across the globe struggling to break the bonds of mass misery, we pledge our best efforts to help them help themselves, for whatever period is required—not because the Communists may be doing it, not because we seek their votes, but because it is right. If a free society cannot help the many who are poor, it cannot save the few who are rich.

To our sister republics south of our border, we offer a special pledge—to convert our good words into good deeds, in a new Alliance for Progress, to assist free men and free governments in casting off the chains of poverty. But this peaceful revolution of hope cannot become the prey of hostile powers. Let all our neighbors know that we shall join with them to oppose aggression or subversion anywhere in the Americas. And let every other power know that this hemisphere intends to remain the master of its own house. . . .

Finally, to those nations who would make themselves our adversary, we offer not a pledge but a request: that both sides begin anew the quest for peace, before the dark powers of destruction unleashed by science engulf all humanity in planned or accidental self-destruction.

So let us begin anew—remembering on both sides that civility is not a sign of weakness, and sincerity is always subject to proof. Let us never negotiate out of fear. But let us never fear to negotiate. . . .

All this will not be finished in the first hundred days. Nor will it be finished in the first thousand days, nor in the life of this administration, nor even perhaps in our lifetime on this planet. But let us begin. . . .

And so, my fellow Americans, ask not what your country can do for you; ask what you can do for your country.

My fellow citizens of the world: Ask not what America will do for you, but what together we can do for the freedom of man. . . .

• *John F. Kennedy delivered his Inaugural Address on 20 January 1961. At the inauguration, Chief Justice Earl Warren administered the oath of office, and Robert Frost read a poem at the ceremony.*

Americans were further pleased that Washington was becoming a more exciting city. The President's witty, beautiful, and socially connected wife, Jacqueline Bouvier, added to that impression.

DOMESTIC POLICY. On the most important domestic issue of the time, that of civil rights, Kennedy could not be counted as much of a liberal on the basis of his record. Nor, for that matter, could most Democrats. The civil rights struggles of the 1950s had received only marginal help from the Democrats. For much of Kennedy's short presidency, the civil rights movement was the work of

President Kennedy was joined outside the door to the Oval Office by his two brothers, Attorney General Robert F. Kennedy (left) and Senator Edward M. Kennedy. (Courtesy John F. Kennedy Library and Museum.)

African American activists along with a number of white allies, all of whom were ready to go to prison or face racist violence along with their African American companions. However, the civil rights forces needed all the federal help they could get, notably in Mississippi, where they were desperately in need of physical protection. Attorney General Robert Kennedy supported voter registration in Mississippi, but he tried to keep the Civil Rights Commission from holding hearings in the state. The Democratic Party was afraid of angering its traditional white southern supporters.

Yet, even as hesitant follower rather than leader, Kennedy did lend far more support to civil rights

than had any of his predecessors, if only because the movement gave occasions for him to do so. During his presidential campaign he had made a phone call to Coretta Scott King while her husband, the great civil rights leader Dr. Martin Luther King, Jr., was imprisoned in Georgia, and Robert Kennedy telephoned the judge in an effort to get King released. Early in his administration, the President appointed a number of African Americans to high positions. He appointed Robert C. Weaver to the Housing and Home Finance Agency. Weaver later became the first African American cabinet officer, the secretary of Housing and Urban Development (HUD), in the administration of Lyndon B. Johnson.

During the 1961 freedom rides in the South, Robert Kennedy made some effort to protect the demonstrators against violence, though he did not put the full weight of the administration behind the freedom riders. When an African American, James Meredith, tried to enroll at the University of Mississippi in 1962, he was met by white mobs. President Kennedy and Attorney General Robert Kennedy sent troops who rescued besieged federal marshals and protected Meredith as he enrolled. Hesitant to act on a campaign pledge to forbid segregation in federally financed housing, the President finally signed a limited order to that effect. In 1963, at a time of especially ugly white violence during civil rights demonstrations in Birmingham, Alabama, Kennedy called for major civil rights legislation, which was passed soon after his assassination. Burke Marshall of the civil rights division of the Justice Department talked Birmingham's business leaders into supporting jobs for African Americans in that city.

In these ways, the Kennedy administration publicly identified itself with the cause of civil rights. An element in that identification was the Kennedy style. The appearance of vigor and confidence, the sense that the President represented the country's intelligence and energy and forces for progress, enabled him to preside over a movement that captured the best implications of the country's heritage.

On other domestic issues, Kennedy's presidency was at least moderately progressive. He proposed a major tax cut to stimulate economic growth. That legislation was passed by the House of Representatives in September 1963 and the Senate soon after his death. Various pilot programs undertaken by his administration became influential in Lyndon B. Johnson's war on poverty, begun the year after Kennedy's death. The President endorsed the idea of a youth conservation corps, and he got Congress to vote for a public works program similar to the New Deal Works Progress Administration. He also addressed the problem of the unequal treatment of women. Kennedy's encouragement and financial support of the space program, with its commitment to the creative powers of modern science and technology, was very much in the spirit of the liberalism of the era. In one of the angriest moments of his administration, he brought massive pressure on the steel industry to roll back a planned price increase.

FOREIGN POLICY. Kennedy is best remembered for foreign policy. He was most in accord with the liberalism of his time in this area. Like other Democrats, he was eager for the United States to increase its global role. He was most militant in pursuing cold war objectives. He was, however, prepared to recognize divisions in the communist world that right-wingers denied or found inconsistent with their concept of massive, unified international communism.

The first large international crisis of Kennedy's presidency was in fact a continuation of plans made by the previous Republican administration: the poorly planned invasion of Cuba, at the Bay of Pigs, by a force of Cuban exiles in April 1961. Seeing that the invasion was doomed, Kennedy was wise enough not to attempt last-minute air intervention. A sequel to the disaster was a determination on the part of the administration to overthrow Cuba's dictator, Fidel Castro, who was friendly with the Soviet Union. The problem of Cuba increased Kennedy's interest in Latin America. That interest was expressed in the Alliance for Progress, a pro-

gram much in the activist mood of the time. This program considered heavy spending to relieve poverty, along with efforts to get recipient governments in Latin America to provide a greater degree of social justice to their citizens. Both objectives combined genuine social concerns with an equally genuine wish to halt the spread of communism.

The Alliance for Progress was a variation of two other ideas of the Kennedy presidency, the Peace Corps, headed by Kennedy's brother-in-law Sargent Shriver, and the Special Forces, better known as the Green Berets. Both trusted in the effectiveness and the fundamental value of expertise. The Peace Corps involved the technical crafts of teachers and farming experts; the Special Forces involved the skills of the military. The Special Forces were supposed to be sensitive also to the local cultures and communities to which they might be sent. The Special Forces and, in a very different way, the Peace Corps exemplified, at the moment of their conception, what the President represented to most Americans: education, schooled ability, a certain grace of style, fearlessness, and a belief that people, young and old, could make a positive difference in the world.

The administration reached an agreement with Premier Nikita Khrushchev of the Soviet Union during a June 1961 summit conference in Vienna, Austria. The conference defused a crisis in Laos that might have involved U.S. troops fighting on the side of an anti-communist group in that country in Southeast Asia. Nevertheless, after the Bay of Pigs, the administration's two largest confrontations were with the Soviet Union.

Except for producing the temporary settlement regarding Laos, the Vienna summit was an unproductive meeting. There, Khrushchev demanded that the West acknowledge the independent status of Soviet-controlled East Germany. Germany had been divided at the end of World War II into four sections, each administered by one of the four major Allies—the United States, the Soviet Union, France, and Great Britain. After Vienna, the Western allies worried that East Germany, with the

Ich bin ein Berliner
(I am a Berliner)

. . . Two thousand years ago the proudest boast was "civis Romanus sum." (I am a Roman citizen.) Today, in the world of freedom, the proudest boast is "Ich bin ein Berliner." (I am a Berliner.) . . .

There are many people in the world who really don't understand, or say they don't, what is the great issue between the free world and the communist world. Let them come to Berlin. There are some who say that communism is the wave of the future. Let them come to Berlin. And there are some who say in Europe and elsewhere we can work with the communists. Let them come to Berlin. And there are even a few who say that it is true that communism is an evil system, but it permits us to make economic progress. . . . Let them come to Berlin.

Freedom has many difficulties and democracy is not perfect, but we have never had to put a wall up to keep our people in, to prevent them from leaving us. . . . While the wall is the most obvious and vivid demonstration of the failures of the communist system, for all the world to see, we take no satisfaction in it, for it is, as your Mayor has said, an offense not only against history but an offense against humanity, separating families, dividing husbands and wives and brothers and sisters, and dividing a people who wish to be joined together. . . .

Freedom is indivisible, and when one man is enslaved, all are not free. . . .

All free men, wherever they may live, are citizens of Berlin, and, therefore, as a free man, I take pride in the words "Ich bin ein Berliner."

President Kennedy gave his famous speech in Berlin at the Rudolph Wilde Platz outside the city hall on 26 June 1963. (Courtesy John F. Kennedy Library and Museum.)

support of the Soviet Union, might absorb the whole of the city of Berlin. Berlin was located within the Soviet sector but was itself divided into four zones, one for each of the victorious Allies. In the early summer of 1961, the communists stopped the flow of East Germans to West Berlin, threatening the economy of Eastern Europe. In August the Berlin wall went up. Kennedy's reaction

---

A STEP TOWARD PEACE

I speak to you tonight in a spirit of hope. Eighteen years ago the advent of nuclear weapons changed the course of the world as well as the war. Since that time, all mankind has been struggling to escape from the darkening prospect of mass destruction on earth. In an age when both sides have come to possess enough nuclear power to destroy the human race several times over, the world of communism and the world of free choice have been caught up in a vicious circle of conflicting ideology and interest. Each increase of tension has produced an increase of arms; each increase of arms has produced an increase of tension. . . .

Yesterday a shaft of light cut into the darkness. Negotiations were concluded in Moscow on a treaty to ban all nuclear tests in the atmosphere, in outer space, and under water. For the first time, an agreement has been reached on bringing the forces of nuclear destruction under international control—a goal first sought in 1946 when Bernard Baruch presented a comprehensive control plan to the United Nations. . . .

• *A treaty banning the testing of nuclear weapons in the atmosphere and in the ocean was concluded on 25 July 1963. President Kennedy announced the provisions of the treaty to the nation the next day.*

---

was to balance force with restraint. He pledged himself to the defense of West Berlin, declaring, during an emotional speech in Berlin, "Ich bin ein Berliner" (I am a Berliner). He reinforced U.S. troops in the city, and later that year a brief face-off between Soviet and U.S. forces occurred. At the same time, he made it clear that he would not attempt to defy the communists' act of sealing off East Germany with a wall.

A greater confrontation between the Soviet Union and the United States took place in October 1962, when Kennedy ordered a naval blockade of Cuba. This was in response to the discovery that the Soviet Union was installing ballistic missiles on the island that could reach the United States. The blockade caused the Soviets to turn back their ships. The blockade actually was a compromise, carefully worked out in secret talks within the administration between those who wanted a military strike against the missile sites and those who proposed that the United States should, in effect, accept their existence. Delicate negotiations had been going on between Moscow and Washington. The negotiations led to the withdrawal of the weapons. In return, the United States agreed not to invade the island and to remove some nearly obsolete missiles from Turkey. The avoidance of war through diplomacy and restraint in the use of force was the major accomplishment of the Kennedy administration.

Then came the first major easing of relations since the initiation of the cold war between the Western and the Soviet blocs. It was, in large degree, a reaction to the Cuban missile crisis. A direct line of communication—the so-called "hot line"—between the White House and the Kremlin (the location of Soviet leadership) was established to provide instant communication in the event of danger. Kennedy and Khrushchev made harmonious, compatible statements and worked out a treaty, ratified by the Senate after Kennedy's death, banning above-ground testing of nuclear explosives. This work of one of the most aggressively global of presidents was predictably defined as appeasement by the political right.

The most obviously unfinished—in retrospect, barely begun—issue of the time was Vietnam. The war there between communist North Vietnam and U.S.-backed South Vietnam never became a central issue of Kennedy's presidency. The administration's deepest involvement was to arrange, in the autumn of 1963, a military coup against the troublesome and corrupt South Vietnamese regime of Ngo Dinh Diem. Against Washington's wishes Diem was immediately murdered by the leaders of the coup. Kennedy increased the number of U.S. advisory and support troops in South Vietnam but hoped for no huge engagement. Having brought a measure of détente (easing of tensions) in Europe, Kennedy died on the eve of the nation's largest and most disastrous effort of the cold war.

"Kennedy began 1963 believing that his 1964 Republican opponent would be Governor Nelson Rockefeller of New York (right) or Senator Barry Goldwater of Arizona (above). He looked forward to the campaign, saying of Rocky: 'No guts,' and of Barry: 'No brains.'" Richard Reeves, President Kennedy, Profile of Power. (Courtesy John F. Kennedy Library and Museum.)

ASSASSINATION AND LEGACY. An assassin's bullet took the life of President Kennedy on 22 November 1963 in Dallas, Texas. The evidence indicates that the assassin was Lee Harvey Oswald, a loner hostile to the foreign policy of the United States Government. Questions remain about the assassination because, among other reasons, Oswald was himself killed very soon after his arrest. In any event, the violent and still mysterious death of President Kennedy has kept him, in the public memory, the romantic figure that his life and his political admirers had already made of him.

President John F. Kennedy's legacy was one of inspiration, particularly to the young, more than of concrete accomplishment, limited by his brief time in the White House. The Peace Corps's hundred thousand volunteers with a median age of 24 years are the finest emblems of Kennedy's legacy. By respecting the cultures of their host nations, those members of the Peace Corps built a good will that is as impossible to measure as is President Kennedy's effect upon an entire generation. Recent public opinion polls have revealed John Fitzgerald Kennedy to be one of the most loved and admired of all the presidents of the United States.

VICE PRESIDENT

Lyndon Baines Johnson
(1908–1973)

CHRONOLOGICAL EVENTS

1908	Born, Stonewall, Texas, 27 August
1930	Graduated from Southwest Texas State Teachers College, San Marcos
1937	Elected to U.S. House of Representatives
1948	Elected to U.S. Senate
1953	Elected Senate minority leader
1955	Elected Senate majority leader
1960	Elected vice president
1963	Became president upon the death of John F. Kennedy
1964	Elected president
1973	Died, Austin, Texas, 22 January

BIOGRAPHY

For Lyndon B. Johnson the vice presidency was an unhappy waiting period between two powerful posts. He was the son of a promising Texas legislator who had been forced out of politics by business debts. Johnson worked his way through Southwest Texas State Teachers College and was hired as secretary to a new U.S. representative.

Johnson quickly learned the ways of Congress. Then he returned to Texas to be state director of the National Youth Administration. He won a special election to the U.S. House of Representatives as a New Deal Democrat.

After losing a race for the U.S. Senate in 1941, he ran again in 1948. His 87-vote victory in a highly disputed race won him the nickname "Landslide Lyndon." Rising rapidly in the Senate Democratic leadership, Johnson became whip, minority leader, and majority leader. Despite a serious heart attack in 1955, he dominated the Senate. His "Johnson treatment" was famous for persuading senators through its mix of sweet talk, threats, and physical contact.

As Democratic leader, Johnson took credit for passing the Civil Rights Act of 1957. He also gave bipartisan support to President Dwight D. Eisenhower on foreign policy. A leading contender for the Democratic presidential nomination in 1960, Johnson avoided the primaries and expected to prevail at the convention. Instead, Senator John F. Kennedy won the primaries and beat Johnson on the first ballot at the convention. After their bitter contest, Kennedy surprised everyone by asking Johnson to run for vice president. Johnson helped Democrats hold the Southern states in a close election.

As vice president, Johnson sought to preside over the Democratic Conference as he had as majority leader. But senators protested this violation of the separation of powers. Johnson found himself similarly excluded from Kennedy's young, Ivy League administration. He seemed to flourish only when he left the country on goodwill missions.

Rumors predicted that Johnson would be dropped from the ticket in 1964, but Kennedy needed him to carry Texas. In November 1963, Kennedy and Johnson were conducting a political tour of Texas when Kennedy was assassinated in Dallas. Johnson took the oath of office on the presidential plane, *Air Force One*, in Dallas.

THE CABINET

SECRETARY OF STATE
Dean Rusk, 1961

SECRETARY OF THE TREASURY
C. Douglas Dillon, 1961

POSTMASTER GENERAL
J. Edward Day, 1961
John A. Gronouski, 1963

ATTORNEY GENERAL
Robert F. Kennedy, 1961

SECRETARY OF THE INTERIOR
Stewart L. Udall, 1961

SECRETARY OF AGRICULTURE
Orville L. Freeman, 1961

SECRETARY OF COMMERCE
Luther H. Hodges, 1961

SECRETARY OF LABOR
Arthur J. Goldberg, 1961
W. Willard Wirtz, 1962

SECRETARY OF DEFENSE
Robert S. McNamara, 1961

SECRETARY OF HEALTH, EDUCATION, AND WELFARE
Abraham A. Ribicoff, 1961
Anthony J. Celebrezze, 1962

Robert F. Kennedy (1925–1968). Kennedy was appointed attorney general by his brother, President John F. Kennedy in 1961. He had previously served as chief counsel of the Senate Select Committee on Improper Activities in the Labor or Management Field. His investigation of the Teamster Union presidents Dave Beck and Jimmy Hoffa uncovered fraud and resulted in the Labor Law Reform Act of 1959.

As attorney general, Kennedy continued to fight against organized crime and labor racketeering. He was an advocate of civil rights, and he strongly enforced voting laws. In 1961, he dispatched federal marshals to protect freedom riders in the South who supported an immediate end to segregation. Kennedy was his brother's closest friend and adviser and played an important role in deliberations during the Cuban missile crisis (1962).

After his brother's assassination, Kennedy resigned his post. In 1964, he successfully ran for the U.S. Senate from New York. A belated candidate for the 1968 Democratic presidential nomination, he attempted to rally the anti-Vietnam forces. On 5 June 1968, almost immediately after acknowledging his victory in the California primary, he was shot by Sirhan Sirhan. He died the following day.

Robert F. Kennedy is shown here with civil rights leaders Martin Luther King, Jr. (left) and Roy Wilkins and Vice President Lyndon B. Johnson (right). 22 June 1963. (Courtesy John F. Kennedy Library and Museum.)

FAMILY

CHRONOLOGICAL EVENTS

28 July 1929	Jacqueline Lee Bouvier born	25 November 1960	Son, John Fitzgerald, born
12 September 1953	Jacqueline Lee Bouvier married John F. Kennedy	22 November 1963	John F. Kennedy died
27 November 1957	Daughter, Caroline, born	19 May 1994	Jacqueline Kennedy Onassis died

John Fitzgerald Kennedy was the second of nine children. He had five sisters and three brothers. This picture was taken on Thanksgiving 1948. Earlier that year, Kathleen (Kick) Kennedy Cavendish, the Marquess of Hartington, had been killed in an airplane accident. Joseph P. Kennedy, a navy pilot, was killed in action during World War II. Rosemary Kennedy was mentally retarded and lived in an institution. The rest of the family is shown here at Hyannis Port in Cape Cod, Massachusetts. From left to right are JFK; Jean; JFK's mother and father, Rose Fitzgerald and Joseph P. Kennedy; Pat; Robert; and Eunice. Kneeling is Edward (Ted) Kennedy. (Courtesy John F. Kennedy Library and Museum.)

(Courtesy John F. Kennedy Library and Museum.)

Jacqueline Bouvier came from a very wealthy family. She made her debut into society in 1947 and graduated from George Washington University four years later. She met John F. Kennedy at a dinner party in 1951. He proposed by telegram in 1953. She was in London photographing the coronation of Queen Elizabeth II. Their wedding reception was a lavish affair at Hammersmith Farms, her stepfather's estate in Newport, Rhode Island.

As First Lady, she brought a feeling of beauty and elegance to the White House. She directed the remodeling of the White House. Five years after the President's assassination, she married Greek shipping multi-millionaire Aristotle Onassis, who died in 1975.

The Kennedys had two children live to maturity. Caroline was six years old when her father died. She graduated from Radcliffe College in 1980, and married Edwin A. Schlossberg in 1987. One year later, she graduated from Columbia University Law School. Caroline Schlossberg has written two books: *In Our Defense* and *The Right to Privacy.*

John F. Kennedy, Jr. graduated from Brown University and New York University Law School. He worked in the office of the district attorney in Manhattan for a few years. In 1996, he became publisher of *George,* a popular magazine with political commentary.

PLACES

JOHN F. KENNEDY NATIONAL HISTORIC SITE

83 Beals Street • Brookline, Massachusetts 02146 • Tel: (617) 566-7937

Located in a suburb of Boston. Open 10 May through 23 October, Wednesday to Sunday, from 10 A.M. to 4:30 P.M. Admission fee, with discounts available. Children ages 15 and under admitted free. Not handicapped accessible. Visitor center located on the lower level. Limited street parking. Administered by the National Park Service, U.S. Department of the Interior.

In 1914, John F. Kennedy's father, Joseph, purchased the three-story house in anticipation of his marriage to Rose Fitzgerald. They moved in after returning from their honeymoon. John was born on 29 May 1917 in the master bedroom.

In 1921, when John was four years old, the Kennedys moved to a larger home a few blocks away at the corner of Abbottsford and Naples roads. The birthplace home was sold to the wife of Edward E. Moore, a close friend and business associate. Over the next 45 years, the home had several owners.

In 1961, the year in which Kennedy was inaugurated as president, the town of Brookline marked the birthplace site with a commemorative plaque. In 1965, two years after his assassination, it was designated a National Historic Landmark. One year later, the Kennedy family repurchased the house for the purpose of restoring it to its 1917 appearance, as a memorial to the late president. In 1967, Congress authorized its inclusion in the National Park System, declaring it a National Historic Site.

The house contains many of the original furnishings that were used by the Kennedy family, including the bed in which President Kennedy was born and the silverware that is marked with his initials. Family photographs and other mementos are also on display.

The house was opened to the public on 29 May 1969. It is shown by guided tour only.

John F. Kennedy's mother, Rose, supervised the restoration of the birthplace home and was able to reacquire approximately 40 percent of the original furnishings. In a letter to the secretary of the interior, she wrote: "It is our intention and hope to make a gift of this home to the American people so that future generations will be able to visit it and see how people lived in 1917 and thus get a better appreciation of the history of this wonderful country." (Courtesy National Park Service; photographer: Richard Frear.)

JOHN F. KENNEDY LIBRARY AND MUSEUM

Columbia Point • Boston, MA 02125 • Tel: (617) 929-4523

Located in the Dorchester section of the city, approximately four miles southeast of downtown Boston. Take I-93 to Exit 14 (northbound) or Exit 15 (southbound). Open daily from 9 A.M. to 5 P.M. The research room is open Monday through Friday from 8:30 A.M. to 4:30 P.M. Call (617) 929-4534 for limited Saturday hours. Closed Thanksgiving, Christmas, and New Year's Day. Admission fee, with discounts available. Children ages 5 and under admitted free. Call in advance for tour information. Museum store and cafe. Handicapped accessible. Administered by the National Archives and Records Administration.

At the dedication ceremony of the new museum in 1993, Senator Edward M. Kennedy stated: "The new museum highlights President Kennedy's fundamental belief that individuals can make a difference, and makes that ideal relevant for today. It is our hope that the museum will be a source of education and inspiration to the Greater Boston community and to visitors throughout the world, and will encourage those who come here to dedicate themselves to public service in their own communities." Approximately 200,000 people visit the library and museum annually. (Courtesy John F. Kennedy Library and Museum.)

The library contains the public and private papers of JFK, his family, and many other prominent individuals who played a major role in the second half of the twentieth century. The collection includes 34 million manuscript pages, 180,000 still photographs, 6 million feet of film and videotape, 1,000 audio tapes, and 15,000 objects. The museum houses 25 exhibits, including re-creations from the 1960 Democratic Convention, and the first televised presidential debate, and of the Oval Office. It also features exhibits on Attorney General Robert F. Kennedy, First Lady Jacqueline Bouvier Kennedy, and other members of the Kennedy family.

The complex, designed by I. M. Pei, is situated on 9.5 acres of the 280-acre Columbia Point peninsula, across from the University of Massachusetts. The 135,000-square-foot library was dedicated on 20 October 1979 by President Jimmy Carter and members of the Kennedy family. The original museum was dedicated in 1979 with the library. The museum exhibits have since been remodeled and enlarged to 18,000 square feet. The new museum was dedicated on 29 October 1993 by President Clinton and members of the Kennedy family.

THE JOHN F. KENNEDY GRAVESITE

Arlington National Cemetery • Arlington, Virginia 22211 • Tel: (703) 692-0931

Located across the Potomac River from Washington, D.C. Can be reached via Arlington Cemetery Metro (blue line). Open daily, April through September, from 8 A.M. to 7 P.M.; October through March, from 8 A.M. to 5 P.M. No admission fee. Visitor center. Handicapped accessible; special car passes available at visitor center. Tours available through Tourmobile and Old Town Trolley.

President Kennedy's gravesite is the single most visited site in Arlington National Cemetery.
(Photograph by A. A. M. van der Heyden.)

President Kennedy's grave is marked by a marble tablet which simply bears his name and birth and death dates. The Eternal Flame is located above his grave. His wife, Jacqueline, lit the flame at his burial service.

The bodies of his wife, Jacqueline, and his two infant children, Patrick and an unnamed baby girl, are buried on either side of him. His brother, Robert, is also buried in Arlington National Cemetery. His gravesite, located a short distance from the President's grave, is marked by a single white cross.

"On December 22, a month after his death, fire from the flame burning at his grave in Arlington was carried at dusk to the Lincoln Memorial. It was fiercely cold. Thousands stood, candles in their hands; then, as the flame spread among us, one candle lighting the next, the crowd gently moved away, the torches flaring and flickering, into the darkness. The next day it snowed—almost as deep a snow as the inaugural blizzard. I went to the White House. It was lovely, ghostly and strange. It all ended, as it began, in the cold."
• Arthur M. Schlesinger, Jr., *A Thousand Days: John F. Kennedy in the White House.*

Lyndon B. Johnson

CHRONOLOGICAL EVENTS

27 August 1908	Born, near Stonewall, Texas
18 August 1930	Graduated from Southwest Texas State Teachers College
1932	Appointed secretary to Texas Congressman Richard M. Kleberg
25 July 1935	Appointed state director of National Youth Administration, Texas
10 April 1937	Elected to U.S. House of Representatives
8 November 1938	Reelected to U.S. House of Representatives
4 November 1941	Defeated for election to U.S. Senate
2 November 1948	Elected to U.S. Senate
2 January 1951	Elected Senate majority whip
3 January 1953	Elected Senate minority leader
2 November 1954	Reelected to U.S. Senate
5 January 1955	Elected Senate majority leader
2 July 1955	Suffered a severe heart attack
8 November 1960	Elected vice president
22 November 1963	Became president upon the death of John F. Kennedy
7 August 1964	Tonkin Gulf Resolution
3 November 1964	Elected president
20 January 1965	Inaugurated president
30 July 1965	Medicare signed into law
30 January 1968	Tet Offensive, Vietnam
31 March 1968	Announced would not run for reelection as president
4 April 1968	Martin Luther King Jr. assassinated
5 June 1968	Robert F. Kennedy assassinated
1969	Retired to the LBJ Ranch, Johnson City, Texas
1971	Published memoirs, *The Vantage Point: Perspectives of the Presidency, 1963–1969*
22 January 1973	Died, Austin, Texas

BIOGRAPHY

Lyndon Baines Johnson, a Democrat from Texas, became the thirty-sixth president of the United States on 22 November 1963. He succeeded John F. Kennedy, following Kennedy's death at the hands of an assassin in Dallas, Texas. Johnson was well-prepared to assume the nation's highest office. He had been a member of Congress for 24 years and Kennedy's vice president for 3 years. After successfully completing the last year of Kennedy's term, he was elected to a full term in 1964. His five-year tenure as president, notable for its failures as well as triumphs, stands as one of the most disturbing and controversial in U.S. history.

Johnson as a young man idolized President Franklin D. Roosevelt, whose liberal social and economic programs revived the nation plagued by the Depression in the 1930s. He, like Roosevelt, believed that the government should play an active role in helping people—particularly the disadvantaged—to improve their lives.

"He was an awesome engine of a man: terrorizing; tender; inexhaustibly energetic; ruthless; loving of land, grass, and water; engulfing; patient; impatient; caring; insightful; devoted to wife, family, and friends; petty; clairvoyant; compassionate; bullying; sensitive; tough; resolute; charming; earthy; courageous; devious; full of humor; brilliantly intelligent; brutal; wise; suspicious; disciplined; crafty; generous . . . He had one goal: to be the greatest president doing the greatest good in the history of the nation. He had one tragedy: a war whose commitments he could not break and whose tenacity he did not perceive." Jack Valenti, A Very Human President. (Courtesy Lyndon B. Johnson Library; photographer: Frank Wolfe.)

On becoming president, Johnson dramatically dedicated his administration to the elimination of poverty in the United States. He proclaimed a national War on Poverty and pushed Congress to enact an array of imaginative programs to provide new advancement opportunities for the poor. He spoke of a future United States without poverty, injustice, or discrimination. Johnson believed he

could unite the country in a common effort to reach what he called a Great Society. Unfortunately, his decision to send increasing numbers of U.S. forces to fight in a bitter conflict in Vietnam, a small country in Southeast Asia, undermined his efforts. His firm pursuit of a war that many Americans opposed divided the nation, eroded his popularity, and eventually forced him into retirement.

EARLY YEARS. Lyndon Johnson was born on 27 August 1908 in the rural hill country of south-central Texas, near the town of Stonewall. He, his brother (Sam III), and his three sisters (Rebekah, Josepha, and Lucia) experienced periods of poverty as they grew up. His father, Sam Ealy Johnson, Jr., was a farmer, cattle trader, and politician who sometimes barely managed to provide for his family. LBJ was five years old when his father gave up farming and moved the family to nearby Johnson City. Outgoing and popular, Sam Johnson was elected five times to the state legislature.

Although Lyndon Johnson learned much about politics from his father, he attributed his success in life largely to his mother, Rebekah Baines Johnson. She, unlike her husband, had been raised in a well-to-do family. Her father was a lawyer and public official. A graduate of Baylor University, Rebekah had hoped to become a writer. She regretted being poor, and she worked tirelessly to educate and instill ambition in her children so that they could have a better life. Johnson told Doris Kearns, one of his biographers: "My mother stressed over and over again that there was nothing, absolutely nothing, that I could not do so long as I had the will to do it and the faith to carry it out."

Despite his mother's intensive tutoring, young Johnson was an indifferent student. He even refused to go to college after graduating from high school in 1924. He eventually enrolled at Southwest Texas State Teachers College to please his mother. He matured there, making good grades, becoming a student leader, and starring on the debate team.

After graduating from college in 1930, Johnson taught speech and debate at Sam Houston High School in Houston, Texas. He was, by all accounts, an imaginative and popular teacher, but politics was in his blood. In his spare time, he worked to elect Richard M. Kleberg to the U.S. House of Representatives. He accepted Kleberg's invitation to go to Washington to become his secretary in 1932.

CONGRESSIONAL SECRETARY. Smart and ambitious, Johnson proved invaluable to Kleberg, who was frequently away from his office. Kleberg gladly allowed his young assistant to run the office, answer mail, represent him in meetings, and even decide how he should vote on legislation. Johnson used this opportunity to learn all he could about Congress and its members. He sought out and introduced himself to influential lawmakers, such as Sam Rayburn. Rayburn had served with his father in the Texas legislature. Johnson's brashness impressed other secretaries. They elected him "Speaker" of their secretarial organization, which was called the Little Congress.

In 1934, Johnson married Claudia Alta "Lady Bird" Taylor, daughter of a prosperous merchant living in Karnack, Texas. A childhood nurse had once said that Claudia was as pretty "as a lady bird," and the name stuck. Her gentle nature and sound judgment in politics and business contributed much to her husband's advancement. While raising their two daughters (Lynda Bird and Luci Baines), she doubled as his trusted political adviser. She also helped him acquire and manage the various business properties through which the couple amassed a personal fortune after World War II.

In 1935, President Roosevelt appointed Johnson to head the Texas office of the National Youth Administration (NYA). The NYA, a new federal agency with offices in every state, was set up to provide public works jobs and vocational training for young people who could not find other employment. Johnson, the youngest NYA administrator in the country, was eager to prove his ability. Within weeks, he assembled a staff and put thousands of young Texans to work on building roads, parks, and schools.

While heading the NYA in Texas, Johnson looked for an opportunity to run for Congress. In 1937, the

representative of his congressional district died. Johnson, along with several more experienced contenders, eagerly campaigned for the vacant seat. Running as the only supporter of Roosevelt in the race, he easily defeated his more conservative opponents.

U.S. REPRESENTATIVE. Johnson entered the U.S. House of Representatives with advantages over most first-term congressmen. He knew his way around Capitol Hill, and he had met many of the leaders of Congress. As an ardent Roosevelt supporter, he had caught the President's eye. Roosevelt took a personal interest in the Texan and made him welcome at the White House. At Roosevelt's insistence, House leaders bypassed more-senior lawmakers in order to appoint him to the Naval Affairs Committee. Johnson sought to move to the U.S. Senate in 1941 but he was defeated by Governor W. Lee O'Daniel in a special election.

Johnson supported Roosevelt's efforts to strengthen the United States's defenses before World War II. When the war began on 7 December 1941, he became the first member of the House of Representatives to volunteer for military service. He came under enemy fire while serving as a lieutenant commander in the Pacific. He was awarded a Silver Star for bravery. In July 1942, at the President's order, he left the U.S. Navy and returned to his congressional duties.

U.S. SENATOR. After 11 years in the House of Representatives, Johnson was elected to the U.S. Senate in 1948. Approaching the job with determination, he studied the Senate's strengths and weaknesses. He mastered its rules. He made friends with its leaders, and volunteered for extra work. Senate leaders rewarded him with a prized seat on the Committee on Armed Services. There, he was a forceful advocate for a strong national defense program and efforts to resist the spread of communism.

In 1951, Senate Democrats elected Johnson to the important leadership job of party whip. As whip, he rounded up votes on key party issues and assisted the party leader. He impressed Democratic majority leader Ernest McFarland with his mastery of the rules and his ability to communicate with various party groups. A Republican landslide in 1952 swept many Democrats, including McFarland, out of office. Senate Democrats lost their majority as well as their leader. Seeking new leadership, they turned to the capable junior senator from Texas.

As minority leader, Johnson opposed efforts of the new Republican administration to cut back Democratic social programs. He did, however, support most of President Dwight D. Eisenhower's foreign actions. He believed that the president should speak for the nation on international matters and that arguing over his decisions weakens the interests of the United States abroad. Johnson's efforts to curb the Democratic criticism of the administration's foreign policy throughout the 1950s troubled many Democrats who preferred an open debate on the president's program. Looking back on that period, some historians have faulted Johnson and his party in Congress for not delving deeper into Eisenhower's policies, particularly his 1955 commitment to send U.S. military advisers to South Vietnam.

MAJORITY LEADER. The voters returned the Democrats to power in both houses in 1954. Johnson became leader of the Senate majority. Besides heading his own party, he was now responsible for managing the day-to-day operations of the entire Senate. He scheduled bills for debate, prodded the Senate to complete its agenda, and negotiated the unanimous-consent agreements which allow the Senate to function efficiently. He performed those tasks with extraordinary skill and success.

His power of persuasion was impressive. Few senators could resist his appeal for a deal, vote, or favor. A big and tall man (six-foot-four), he loomed large over most of his colleagues. His manner could be intimidating. He would stare down into the face of his quarry, drawing so close that noses almost touched. Seeking intimacy with the other person as he talked, he would squeeze an elbow lightly, or drape his arm over a shoulder. His Senate colleagues called it the Johnson treatment. He would argue,

promise, beg, or threaten—whatever it took to have his way.

Johnson pushed the Senate to a level of efficiency it has seldom equaled, before or since. In his first year as majority leader, the Senate passed some 1,300 bills. This was more than in the previous two years combined. After recovering from a severe heart attack in 1955, he helped pass most major laws of the late 1950s. The Civil Rights Act of 1957, the first civil rights law since 1885, and the National Aeronautics and Space Act of 1958 which created the National Aeronautics and Space Administration (NASA) were passed under his leadership.

VICE PRESIDENT. Johnson sought his party's nomination for president in 1960. Democrats passed him over, however, for the relatively inexperienced Senator John F. Kennedy of Massachusetts. After some hesitancy, Johnson accepted Kennedy's invitation to join him on the party ticket as the vice-presidential nominee.

In November, Kennedy narrowly defeated his Republican opponent, Richard M. Nixon, 34,227,096 votes to 34,107,646 votes. Many Democrats attributed their party's victory to Kennedy's running mate, whose background as a politically moderate southerner helped Kennedy, a northern liberal, win in several Southern states crucial to his election.

Johnson was never comfortable in the subordinate role of vice president. Kennedy gave him too few assignments for his liking. He spent much of his time on Capitol Hill, fulfilling his official duties as president and chief presiding officer of the Senate.

Johnson chaired two executive committees for Kennedy: the President's Committee on Equal Employment Opportunity and the National Aeronautics and Space Council. The space council was responsible for fulfilling a Kennedy pledge to land an American on the moon by 1970. Having once headed the Senate Committee on Aeronautical and Space Sciences, Johnson was familiar with the problems of space-program development. His knowledge contributed significantly to the success of the moon-landing project, known as the Apollo mission.

Johnson represented President Kennedy on several missions abroad. In May 1961, he met with President Ngo Dinh Diem of South Vietnam, whose government was engaged in a violent civil war against a guerrilla army, backed by communist North Vietnam. He assured Diem that the United States would continue to support his efforts to defeat the guerrillas. Some 600 U.S. military personnel were then serving as advisers to the South Vietnamese army. Johnson concluded that U.S. troops were neither needed nor wanted in South Vietnam, except as trainers and advisers. He warned Kennedy, however, that the United States eventually would have to consider expanding U.S. military involvement, or "cut our losses and withdraw should our efforts fail."

PRESIDENT. A joint political appearance brought President Kennedy and Vice President Johnson to Dallas in November 1963. Welcoming crowds lined the streets as they rode in separate open cars through the downtown area. As their parade of automobiles turned on to Elm Street, (according the official findings called the Warren Commission Report), a lone gunman, identified as Lee Harvey Oswald, fired several shots at the President from a window of the nearby Texas School Book Depository. One bullet, said the Report, struck Kennedy in the head. He was rushed to a nearby hospital. The car bearing the vice president also sped to the hospital. There, Johnson learned that Kennedy was dead. In the confusion, he did not take the oath of office until later that afternoon. A federal judge administered the oath aboard the presidential plane *Air Force One*, as it prepared to transport Kennedy's body back to Washington.

Johnson won praise for his conduct as president during the critical days following Kennedy's assassination. His confidence and sound decisions reassured a nation eager to know that, despite the shocking loss of its popular leader, the government remained in capable hands.

The press labeled Johnson "the Great Conciliator," referring to his efforts to reach out to all segments of society. His gestures of friendship and coopera-

Federal District Judge Sarah Tilghman Hughes administered the presidential oath to Lyndon Baines Johnson on board Air Force One, *after the assassination of President Kennedy. He is flanked by Jacqueline Kennedy (right) and Lady Bird Johnson.*
(Courtesy Lyndon B. Johnson Library; photographer: Cecil Stoughton.)

tion extended to business and labor leaders, groups representing African American and other minorities, and many others. He flattered various leaders by seeking their help and advice. He used his good offices to settle a railroad labor strike that had dragged on for five years. As a result, his reputation as a peacemaker soared. Johnson's concern for economy in government pleased taxpayers. They applauded when he scolded his own White House staff for wasting electricity and ordered that the lights throughout the mansion be switched off when not needed.

Most of Kennedy's legislative proposals were stalled in Congress when he died. Johnson pledged, as a tribute to the late president, to press for speedy passage of those bills. Under his persuasion, Congress passed nearly all the major bills within the next few months, including a civil rights law to combat discrimination in hiring and also in access to public facilities; an Urban Mass Transportation Act to improve bus, rail, and other public-transit services; a tax-reduction measure; and several environmental laws.

Unlike Kennedy, who had focused on foreign affairs, Johnson planned to concentrate on domes-

Soon after he became president, Lyndon B. Johnson met with civil rights leaders (from left to right) Martin Luther King Jr., Whitney Young, and James Farmer. As Senate majority leader, Johnson had masterminded the first civil rights law to pass Congress in almost a century. As president, he secured passage of a law that guaranteed the voting rights of all Americans. (Courtesy Lyndon B. Johnson Library; photographer: Yoichi R. Okamoto.)

tic issues. He unveiled his own vision of America's future in a speech at the University of Michigan on 22 May 1964. "In your time," he told the student audience," we have the opportunity to move not only toward the rich society and the powerful society, but upward to the Great Society. The Great Society rests on abundance and liberty for all. It demands an end to poverty and racial injustice to which we are totally committed in our time. But that is just the beginning."

An array of proposed legislation followed this speech. It was labeled collectively as Johnson's Great Society program. The Economic Opportunity Act of 1964 was the first of those measures to clear Congress. It created an Office of Economic Opportunity to oversee 10 antipoverty programs. These programs included a Job Corps to give young people work experience and training; a preschool education program, called Head Start, for disadvantaged children; a program to help communities combat poverty locally; an adult-education program, and a volunteer service program, called VISTA (Volunteers in Service to America) which was a domestic

version of the highly successful Peace Corps.

Impressed by his performance as a caretaker president, and his pledge that Americans would not be sent to fight Asian wars, voters in November 1964 elected Johnson to a full four-year term of his own. Winning 61 percent of the vote, he overwhelmed his Republican opponent, Barry Goldwater. In Congress, the Democrats raised their majorities by 2 seats in the Senate and 38 seats in the House.

Johnson saw the election as a command from the voters to pursue his bold agenda. The fact that the United States was being drawn deeper and deeper into a spreading conflict in Vietnam did not weaken his determination to focus on domestic matters in 1965. Seldom, if ever, has a president matched Johnson's masterly performance that year in dealing with Congress and various special-interest groups.

Under Johnson's constant prodding, Congress passed an extraordinary number of important new laws in 1965. Of the 88 major proposals he sent to Capitol Hill that year, 84 were enacted into law. Among them were:

- The Civil Rights Act of 1965, which banned literacy and other voter-qualification tests

THE GREAT SOCIETY

. . . Your imagination, your initiative, and your indignation will determine whether we build a society where progress is the servant of our needs, or a society where old values and new visions are buried under unbridled growth. For in your time we have the opportunity to move not only toward the rich society and the powerful society, but upward to the Great Society.

The Great Society rests on abundance and liberty for all. It demands an end to poverty and racial injustice, to which we are totally committed in our time. But that is just the beginning.

The Great Society is a place where every child can find knowledge to enrich his mind and to enlarge his talents. It is a place where leisure is a welcome chance to build and reflect, not a feared cause of boredom and restlessness. It is a place where the city of man serves not only the needs of the body and the demands of commerce but the desire for beauty and the hunger for community. . . .

But most of all, the Great Society is not a safe harbor, a resting place, a final objective, a finished work. It is a challenge constantly renewed, beckoning us toward a destiny where the meaning of our lives matches the marvelous products of our labor.

So I want to talk to you today about three places where we begin to build the Great Society—in our cities, in our countryside, and in our classrooms.

Many of you will live to see the day, perhaps 50 years from now, when there will be 400 million Americans—four-fifths of them in urban areas. In the remainder of this century urban population will double, city land will double, and we will have to build homes, highways, and facilities equal to all those built since this country was first settled. So in the next 40 years we must rebuild the entire urban United State. . . .

Our society will never be great until our cities are great. Today the frontier of imagination and innovation is inside those cities and not beyond their borders. . . .

A second place where we begin to build the Great Society is in our countryside. We have always prided ourselves on being not only America the strong and America the free, but America the beautiful. Today that beauty is in danger. The water we drink, the food we eat, the very air that we breathe, are threatened with pollution. Our parks are overcrowded, our seashores overburdened. Green fields and dense forests are disappearing. . . .

A third place to build the Great Society is in the classrooms of American. There your children's lives will be shaped. Our society will not be great until every young mind is set free to scan the farthest reaches of thought and imagination. We are still far from that goal. . . .

In many places, classrooms are overcrowded and curricula are outdated. Most of our qualified teachers are underpaid, and many of our paid teachers are unqualified. So we must give every child a place to sit and a teacher to learn from. Poverty must not be a bar to learning, and learning must offer an escape from poverty.

But more classrooms and more teachers are not enough. We must seek an educational system which grows in excellence as it grows in size. This means better training for our teachers. It means preparing youth to enjoy their hours of leisure as well as their hours of labor. It means exploring new techniques of teaching, to find new ways to stimulate the love of learning and the capacity for creation.

These are three of the central issues of the Great Society. . . .

• *President Johnson delivered these remarks at the graduation ceremony at the University of Michigan on 22 May 1964.*

that had long kept African Americans from registering to vote in some southern states.

- The Elementary-Secondary Education Act of 1965, which provided federal aid to local school systems for basic education and special programs in low-income areas.

- The Medicare and Medicaid Acts, which established a federal health-insurance program (Medicare) for persons 65 and older, and a free health-care program (Medicaid) for all low-income persons.

- The Higher Education Act, which provided scholarships and low-interest loans for college students; financial aid for small colleges and libraries; and a Teacher Corps, whose participants would assist regular teachers in poor areas.

▲ *Former President Harry S. Truman had retired to Independence, Missouri. President Johnson went there to sign Medicare into law on 30 July 1965. It was Truman who had first proposed this legislation in 1945.* (Courtesy Lyndon B. Johnson Library.)

Other enactments of the Eighty-ninth Congress included an expanded antipoverty program; a rent-supplement program; auto-safety measures; air- and water-pollution controls; a highway-beautification act; and programs to award grants and scholarships for the visual and performing arts, and the humanities.

Johnson's dominance over Congress peaked with the outpouring of new social legislation in 1965.

▲ *Thurgood Marshall was the first African-American Justice of the Supreme Court. President Johnson appointed him in 1967. For 25 years, Marshall had served as a lawyer for the National Association for the Advancement of Colored People (NAACP). In 1961, he left the NAACP when President Kennedy appointed him to the United States Court of Appeals. Four years later, President Johnson nominated him to be his solicitor general.*

Marshall is shown here with Johnson in the Oval Office. He is phoning his wife to tell her that the President has just nominated him to the Supreme Court. (Courtesy Lyndon B. Johnson Library; photographer: Yoichi R. Okamoto.)

Lawmakers who had supported his domestic agenda in 1964 and 1965 became less supportive later, when some of his new programs proved more expensive than expected, and others failed to achieve their goals. In 1967, Congress began to scale back many of the President's Great Society initiatives and to question his requests for still more programs.

In 1966, 1967, and 1968, Congress passed only a handful of the administration's proposals. It did, however, respond to Johnson's call for another major civil rights law, this one barring discrimination in the sale or rental of housing.

VIETNAM. The Vietnam conflict continued to intrude on Johnson's pursuit of a Great Society. On 2 August 1964, the President announced to the nation that North Vietnam gunboats had attacked

SPECIAL MESSAGE TO THE CONGRESS
THE AMERICAN PROMISE

. . . At times history and fate meet at a single time in a single place to shape a turning point in man's unending search for freedom. So it was at Lexington and Concord. So it was a century ago at Appomattox. So it was last week at Selma, Alabama.

There, long-suffering men and women peacefully protested the denial of their rights as Americans. Many were brutally assaulted. One good man, a man of God, was killed.

There is no cause for pride in what has happened in Selma. There is no cause for self-satisfaction in the long denial of equal rights of millions of Americans. But there is cause for hope and for faith in our democracy for what is happening here tonight. . . .

In our time we have come to live with moments of great crisis. Our lives have been marked with debate about great issues; issues of war and peace, issues of prosperity and depression. But rarely in any time does an issue lay bare the secret heart of America itself. Rarely are we met with a challenge, not to our growth or abundance, our welfare or our security, but rather to the values and the purposes and the meaning of our beloved Nation.

The issue of equal rights for American Negroes is such an issue. And should we defeat every enemy, should we double our wealth and conquer the stars, and still be unequal to this issue, then we will have failed as a people and as a nation. . . .

There is no Negro problem. There is no Southern problem. There is no Northern problem. There is only an American problem. And we are met here tonight as Americans—not as Democrats or Republicans—we are met here as Americans to solve that problem. . . .

There is no constitutional issue here. The command of the Constitution is plain.

There is no moral issue. It is wrong—deadly wrong—to deny any of your fellow Americans the right to vote in this country.

There is no issue of States rights or national rights. There is only the struggle for human rights. . . .

But even if we pass this bill, the battle will not be over. What happened in Selma is part of a far larger movement which reaches into every section and State of America. It is the effort of American Negroes to secure for themselves the full blessings of American life.

Their cause must be our cause too. Because it is not just Negroes, but really it is all of us, who must overcome the crippling legacy of bigotry and injustice.

And we shall overcome. . . .

• *President Johnson delivered this speech to a joint session of Congress on 15 March 1965.*
"A march in Alabama to dramatize the disenfranchisement of black people in that state was set upon outside Selma by mobs and state troopers with gas and clubs and whips in a confrontation destined to become etched in the nation's memory. Riding the crest of public horror and indignation at the brutality and terror unleashed against the marchers, Johnson went before the Congress to make one of the most impassioned speeches of his career. . . . Roy Wilkins, head of the NAACP, said later that the galleries were leaning forward, because 'the President was beginning to speak as we had heard no President speak before.' When he capped his plea for justice with the thundering words of the civil rights movement—'We shall overcome'—the chamber exploded in a roar of affirmation that seemed to signal an end forever to the old order of race relations." Harry Middleton, LBJ: The White House Years.

two U.S. destroyers in the Gulf of Tonkin. He ordered retaliatory air strikes against North Vietnam and asked Congress to support his action.

Congress, by near-unanimous vote, passed the Tonkin Gulf Resolution on 7 August. It declared the security of Southeast Asia to be a vital national interest of the United States. It also supported the determination of the President "to take all necessary measures," including the use of armed force, to repel any future attacks. Johnson began carrying a copy of the resolution in his pocket, citing it when questioned about his legal authority to expand the role of the United States in the war.

Before 1965, the United States limited its role to advising and training the South Vietnam army. That role changed in February 1965, when communist guerrillas (called Viet Cong) attacked a U.S. barracks near the village of Pleiku. Johnson responded by ordering air strikes against Viet Cong training and staging areas in North Vietnam. With that attack the United States became a full participant in the war.

More Viet Cong attacks were answered with more air strikes until, within months, U.S. bombing missions had become routine. The President and his advisers believed the bombing would force a negotiated settlement. It only strengthened the communists' resolve to fight on. Gradually, Johnson realized that there would be no quick, negotiated end to the conflict. He turned increasingly to a military solution. By year's end, tens of thousands of U.S. soldiers were combing South Vietnam's jungles and villages in search of elusive Viet Cong and North Vietnamese fighting units.

Some 23,000 U.S. soldiers were on duty in South Vietnam at the end of 1964. A year later, the number had swelled to 181,000. It grew to 389,000 in 1966, to 486,000 in 1967, and to 535,000 in 1968. To meet such manpower demands, Johnson had to order the drafting of millions of young men. The massive draft calls created a wave of unrest across the nation, especially on college campuses.

On 24 March 1965, students at the University of Michigan condemned Johnson's policies in a 12-hour marathon of speeches and seminars opposing

When the Prime Minister of Australia died, President Johnson attended the memorial service in Melbourne. On the way home, he stopped in Vietnam to meet with General William Westmoreland. Westmoreland was commander of U.S. troops in Vietnam. (Courtesy Lyndon B. Johnson Library; photographer: Yoichi R. Okamoto.)

the war. The action, called a teach-in, spread to other colleges. Different forms of protest also began to spread widely throughout the year. In October alone, antiwar activists held rallies and marches in some 60 cities. Johnson held his course, even later, when protesters gathered by the thousands outside the White House to chant, "Hey, hey, LBJ, how many kids did you kill today?" The President continued the bombing, and the draft calls continued to climb.

As the war escalated, Johnson found less time for other matters. He began spending hours every day in the White House Situation Room, his command post for gathering war information and issuing orders to the military. On Capitol Hill, supporters of his Vietnam policy began to desert him. The lawmakers divided into two camps—"hawks," who favored Johnson's war policies, and "doves," who opposed U.S. involvement in the war.

Many Americans questioned the war's ever-mounting cost in lives and money. The President insisted that the war was necessary and that the nation could afford the war's cost without cutting back on his domestic programs. Congress spent much of 1966 and 1967 debating that issue without resolving it.

By 1967, Johnson clearly was eager to get the United States out of the war at almost any cost, short of outright withdrawal. National honor, he believed, required that the United States not simply abandon its ally. On that point, he still had the support of Congress and most Americans. He grew increasingly frustrated when intense military pressure did not bring North Vietnam's leaders to the peace table. He tried luring them with various approaches, including bombing pauses and a personal letter to North Vietnam's president, Ho Chi Minh. Ho rejected Johnson's proposal of direct talks.

As if to mock Johnson's peace overtures, the communists launched a surprise offensive in January 1968. The so-called Tet Offensive occurred during Vietnam's Tet holiday period and caught the U.S. and South Vietnamese forces unprepared. Although it failed, the offensive showed that the communists remained strong and resourceful. It also convinced many Americans, including some of Johnson's top advisers, that the United States could not win the war militarily. In terms of popular support for continued U.S. involvement in the conflict, Tet was a disaster for the President.

By 1968, the war had created bitter divisions within the United States. Antiwar protests, most of them directed personally at the President, became increasingly violent. They limited Johnson's ability to travel in some parts of the country and to campaign actively for his own reelection in November. Nevertheless, he won the Democratic presidential primary in New Hampshire, barely defeating Senator Eugene McCarthy. McCarthy inspired young supporters with his antiwar platform.

Johnson never stopped trying to persuade North Vietnam to enter into peace negotiations. He finally succeeded—but at a high personal cost. Addressing the nation on 31 March 1968, he announced that he had ordered a bombing halt over most of North Vietnam. His hope, he said, was that the enemy would show similar restraint. The speech ended with his stunning announcement that he was withdrawing from participation in politics to devote his full time and energy to the quest for peace. He would, he said, neither seek nor accept his party's nomination for another term as president in 1968.

Johnson's dramatic gesture drew a quick response from North Vietnam. Its leaders agreed to open preliminary discussions with the United States in Paris on 13 May 1968. On 31 October 1968, Johnson ordered all bombing halted over North Vietnam. Although many issues remained to be settled at the peace table, he left office believing that the United States's most agonizing war was finally winding down. Events proved him wrong: the war continued with renewed violence for another four years.

RETIREMENT. At the end of his term in January 1969, Johnson returned to Texas. He spent his remaining years living quietly with Mrs. Johnson at their ranch on the Pedernales River, not far from where he was born. In retirement he wrote his memoirs and lived to see the opening of the Lyndon B. Johnson Library and Museum in Austin. He died on 22 January 1973 and was buried in the family cemetery at the ranch.

Lyndon Johnson left office as a tragic figure of history. He had devoted much of his career to the idea of government as a positive force in people's lives. He had worked long and hard to attain the presidency—the ultimate position from which he might do the most good for people. Few presidents have matched the success of his first two years in office. His programs in civil rights, education, welfare, and health enriched the lives of millions of Americans. Yet, history remembers him less for his progress toward a Great Society than for his dogged pursuit of a distant war. However honorable the cause, it was a war that he never really sought to enter and that most Americans never approved of or understood.

Address to the Nation

. . . Tonight I want to speak to you of peace in Vietnam and Southeast Asia.

No other question so preoccupies our people. No other dream so absorbs the 250 million human beings who live in that part of the world. No other goal motivates American policy in Southeast Asia.

For years, representatives of our Government and others have traveled the world—seeking to find a basis for peace talks. . . .

There is no need to delay the talks that could bring an end to this long and this bloody war.

Tonight, I renew the offer I made last August—to stop the bombardment of North Vietnam. We ask that talks begin promptly, that they be serious talks on the substance of peace. We assume that during those talks Hanoi will not take advantage of our restraint.

We are prepared to move immediately toward peace through negotiations.

So, tonight, in the hope that this action will lead to early talks, I am taking the first step to de-escalate the conflict. We are reducing—substantially reducing—the present level of hostilities.

And we are doing so unilaterally, and at once. . . .

Throughout my entire public career I have followed the personal philosophy that I am a free man, an American, a public servant, and a member of my party, in that order always and only.

For 37 years in the service of our Nation, first as a Congressman, as a Senator, and as Vice President, and now as your President, I have put the unity of the people first. I have put it ahead of any divisive partisanship.

And in these times as in times before, it is true that a house divided against itself by the spirit of faction, of party, of region, of religion, of race, is a house that cannot stand.

There is division in the American house now. There is divisiveness among us all tonight. And holding the trust that is mine, as President of all the people, I cannot disregard the peril to the progress of the American people and the hope and prospect of peace for all peoples. . . .

I have concluded that I should not permit the Presidency to become involved in the partisan divisions that are developing in this political year.

With America's sons in the fields far away, with America's future under challenge right here at home, with our hopes and the world's hopes for peace in the balance every day, I do not believe that I should devote an hour or a day of my time to any personal partisan causes or to any duties other than the awesome duties of this office—the Presidency of your country.

Accordingly, I shall not seek, and I will not accept, the nomination of my party for another term as your President.

But let men everywhere know, however, that a strong, a confident, and a vigilant America stands ready tonight to seek an honorable peace—and stands ready tonight to defend an honored cause—whatever the price, whatever the burden, whatever the sacrifice that duty may require.

• *At 9 p.m. on 31 March 1968, President Johnson delivered this Address on national television. In* LBJ: The White House Years, *Harry Middleton, a former assistant to the president, said: "The response throughout the nation was electric. He was hailed by supporters and opponents alike, and his popularity, measured in the polls, rose dramatically."*

VICE PRESIDENT

Hubert Horatio Humphrey
(1911–1977)

CHRONOLOGICAL EVENTS

1911	Born, Wallace, South Dakota, 27 May
1939	Graduated from University of Minnesota
1944	Elected mayor of Minneapolis, Minnesota
1948	Elected to U.S. Senate
1964	Elected vice president
1968	Ran unsuccessfully for president
1970	Again elected to U.S. Senate
1977	Died, Waverly, Minnesota, 13 January

BIOGRAPHY

Hubert Humphrey was born in South Dakota, where his father ran a drug store. After attending the University of Minnesota, Humphrey returned to work in the store. He did graduate studies in political science and then took a post with the Works Progress Administration, a New Deal agency. He was elected mayor of Minneapolis, with organized labor's backing.

Humphrey first achieved national notice in 1948 when he proposed a strong civil rights plank at the Democratic convention. Adoption of the plank caused some Southern delegates to walk out in protest. When Humphrey won a seat in the U.S. Senate, Southern senators at first shunned him. But he was befriended by Texas Senator Lyndon B. Johnson. Under Johnson's guidance, Humphrey changed his style and gained acceptance among his colleagues.

Following an unsuccessful bid for the presidency in 1960, Humphrey became Senate Democratic whip. He was floor manager for the Civil Rights Act of 1964 and sponsored a long list of other liberal reforms. President Lyndon Johnson then tapped him to run for vice president.

Humphrey shared Johnson's vision of a "Great Society" and lobbied Congress for enactment of his sweeping legislative program. But the Vice President felt troubled over the expanding U.S. military intervention in Vietnam. When Humphrey privately advocated a bombing halt and a negotiated peace settlement, Johnson shut him out of the administration's decision making. To regain Johnson's confidence, Humphrey became a defender of the war.

His shift from "dove" to "hawk" restored Humphrey's standing with Johnson but hurt him in the eyes of Democratic liberals. In 1968, after Johnson withdrew from the race and New York Senator Robert F. Kennedy was assassinated, Humphrey received the Democratic nomination for president. Violent clashes between antiwar demonstrators and Chicago police outside the convention hall contradicted Humphrey's "politics of joy." He narrowly lost the presidency to the Republican nominee, Richard M. Nixon.

Humphrey briefly taught in Minnesota until he won another term in the Senate. He tried unsuccessfully for the presidential nomination in 1972 and 1976 and lost a race to become Senate majority leader. News that he was terminally ill with cancer prompted an outpouring of national affection. A joint session of Congress celebrated the valiant, if not always successful, public career of the "Happy Warrior."

THE CABINET

SECRETARY OF STATE
Dean Rusk, 1963, 1965

SECRETARY OF THE TREASURY
C. Douglas Dillon, 1963, 1965
Henry H. Fowler, 1965
Joseph W. Barr, 1968

POSTMASTER GENERAL
John A. Gronouski, Jr., 1963, 1965
Lawrence F. O'Brien, 1965
W. Marvin Watson, 1968

ATTORNEY GENERAL
Robert F. Kennedy, 1963
Nicholas deB. Katzenbach, 1965
Ramsey Clark, 1967

SECRETARY OF THE INTERIOR
Stewart L. Udall, 1963, 1965

SECRETARY OF AGRICULTURE
Orville L. Freeman, 1963, 1965

SECRETARY OF COMMERCE
Luther H. Hodges, 1963
John T. Connor, 1965
Alexander B. Trowbridge, 1967
C.R. Smith, 1968

SECRETARY OF LABOR
W. Willard Wirtz, 1963, 1965

SECRETARY OF DEFENSE
Robert S. McNamara, 1963, 1965
Clark Clifford, 1968

SECRETARY OF HEALTH, EDUCATION, AND WELFARE
Anthony J. Celebrezze, 1963, 1965
John W. Gardner, 1965
Wilbur J. Cohen, 1968

SECRETARY OF HOUSING AND URBAN DEVELOPMENT1
Robert C. Weaver, 1966
Robert C. Wood, 1969

SECRETARY OF TRANSPORTATION2
Alan S. Boyd, 1967

1. Department of Housing and Urban Development established 9 September 1965.
2. Department of Transportation established 1 April 1967.

Nicholas deB. Katzenbach (right) is shown with President Lyndon B. Johnson. The President is announcing the arrest of Ku Klux Klan members suspected of murdering James Reeb, a white Unitarian minister from Boston, on the road between Selma and Montgomery, Alabama. (Courtesy Lyndon Baines Johnson Library; photographer: Yoichi R. Okamoto.)

Nicholas deB. Katzenbach (1922–). Katzenbach was appointed assistant attorney general by President John F. Kennedy in 1961. He was promoted to deputy attorney general in 1962 and was appointed attorney general by President Lyndon B. Johnson in 1965.

Katzenbach was a strong advocate of civil rights in both the Kennedy and Johnson administrations. In 1962, as deputy attorney general, Katzenbach headed the Justice Department team which was sent to the University of Mississippi to enforce the admission of the first African American student. The following year, he personally escorted the first African American students to enroll at the University of Alabama.

Katzenbach helped draft the Civil Rights Act of 1964 and the Voting Rights Act of 1965. His name appears in the Supreme Court cases, *Katzenbach v. McClung* (1964) and *Katzenbach v. Morgan* (1966). These decisions upheld the constitutionality of the Civil Rights Act of 1964 and the Voting Rights Act of 1965, respectively. Katzenbach served as attorney general until 1966, when President Johnson appointed him undersecretary of state.

President Lyndon B. Johnson is shown here with Secretary of Defense Robert S. McNamara (far left), Ambassador to the Soviet Union Averell W. Harriman, and Secretary of State Dean Rusk (right). (Courtesy Lyndon Baines Johnson Library; photographer: Yoichi R. Okamoto.)

Robert S. McNamara (1916–). McNamara was appointed secretary of defense by President John F. Kennedy in 1961 and was reappointed by President Lyndon B. Johnson in 1964.

McNamara directed the escalation of the Vietnam War. In Spring 1964, Senator Wayne Morse of Oregon bitterly referred to Vietnam as "McNamara's War." Following McNamara's advice, Johnson committed more than half a million U.S. troops in the conflict by 1967. He retired in 1967. The following year, he became president of the World Bank.

Dean Rusk (b. 1909). Rusk was appointed secretary of state by President John F. Kennedy in 1961 and was reappointed by President Lyndon B. Johnson in 1964.

Rusk strongly supported U.S. involvement in Vietnam. He advised President Johnson to send additional ground forces in 1965. Two years later, he asserted that the U.S. had begun to win the war. By the end of the Johnson administration, however, Rusk was harshly criticized for focusing too much of his attention on the war in Vietnam and not on U.S. relations with the Soviet Union and Third World nations.

FAMILY

CHRONOLOGICAL EVENTS

22 December 1912	Claudia Alta (Lady Bird) Taylor born	19 March 1944	Daughter, Lynda Bird, born
17 November 1934	Lady Bird Taylor married Lyndon Baines Johnson	2 July 1947	Daughter, Luci Baines, born
		22 January 1973	Lyndon Baines Johnson died

Lady Bird is shown here on 31 March 1968 working with the President on his Address to the Nation. Soon after this picture was taken, the President announced his plans to de-escalate the Vietnam War and his intention to not seek another term. (Courtesy Lyndon B. Johnson Library; photographer: Yoichi R. Okamoto.)

Claudia Taylor (Lady Bird) met Lyndon Johnson in 1934, the year she graduated from the University of Texas. He proposed the day after they met, and they were married later that year. She would be his partner, in every sense of the word, for almost 40 years.

In 1942, she invested in a Texas radio station, which she built into a huge communications business. As First Lady, she will be remembered for her support of the Highway Beautification Act, which limited billboards and junkyards along the nation's highways. She was also a great supporter of the war against poverty, particularly Head Start, which provided for early education for poor children.

She published *White House Diary* in 1970. Lady Bird Johnson lives in Austin and is active in many groups including the LBJ Library and the University of Texas.

▲ *Lynda Bird Johnson (left) married Charles S. Robb, a Captain in the United States Marine Corps, at the White House in 1967. He was governor of Virginia from 1982 to 1986. In 1988, he was elected to the U.S. Senate.*

Luci Baines Johnson (right) married Patrick Nugent in 1966. President Johnson walked her down the aisle at Washington's Shrine of the Immaculate Conception. A large reception at the White House followed. Nineteen-year-old Luci was the first daughter of a president in office to marry since Eleanor Wilson in 1914. They divorced in 1979. She remarried and moved to Toronto, Canada. (Courtesy Lyndon B. Johnson Library.)

Lynda Bird (second from left) and Luci are shown here with their parents after Lyndon's nomination for vice president in Chicago, July 1960. (Courtesy National Archives.) ▶

Lyndon B. Johnson National Historic Park

P.O. Box 329 • Johnson City, Texas 78636 • Tel: (512) 644-2241

Located off U.S. Highway 290 and U.S. Highway 281 in south-central Texas. The Lyndon B. Johnson National Historic Park consists of two distinct units that are 15 miles apart. The first is the Johnson City Unit, which contains the boyhood home, the Johnson settlement, a visitor center, and the park headquarters. The second is the LBJ Ranch Unit, which is part of the Johnson State Historic Park and contains the birthplace house, the Junction School, the Johnson family cemetery, the Texas White House, and a visitor center. Both sites are open daily from 9 A.M. to 5 P.M. Closed Christmas and New Year's Day. No admission fee. The LBJ Ranch Bus Tour is offered daily from 10 A.M. to 4 P.M. except Christmas. It departs from the State Historic Park Visitor Center. Fee, with discounts available for children and school groups. Tour scripts are available for the hearing impaired. Designated Johnson City sites and the LBJ Ranch Bus Tour are wheelchair accessible. The National Historic Park is administered by the National Parks Service, U.S. Department of the Interior. The State Historic Park is administered by the Texas Parks and Wildlife Department.

In January 1964, the Johnson family asked Austin architect J. Roy White to begin the restoration of President Johnson's birthplace. By the end of August 1964, the reconstruction was completed. It was legally transferred to the newly established Lyndon B. Johnson National Historic Site in 1970. (Courtesy National Park Service; photographer: Fred E. Mang, Jr.)

Lyndon B. Johnson was born in a two-bedroom farmhouse on the banks of the Pedernales River, approximately one mile east of the present LBJ Ranch site. In 1913, when he was five years old, his family moved to Johnson City. The birthplace house was occupied until 1935, when it was torn down and a smaller house was built with some of the materials from the original. In 1964, the second house was still intact when the Johnson family decided to reconstruct the birthplace. Some materials from the original structure were used for the reconstruction. It is now part of the Johnson State Historic Park.

In 1913, the Johnson family moved into a modest 1901 frame house one block off of Main Street in Johnson City. LBJ lived there for the next 22 years.

In 1964, the boyhood home was extensively remodeled and was restored to the period of 1922 to 1925. The roof was covered with red cedar shingles, the sitting area in the east porch was rebuilt, and the original wallpaper design was reproduced. Much of the original pine flooring and beaded ceiling wood was retained. It is now part of the Johnson National Historic Park.

In 1951, Johnson purchased a ranch at Stonewall from his aunt. During his presidency, the ranch house, known as the Texas White House, became an international attraction and a center of political activity. It housed an elaborate communications and security system and a private airstrip. In 1972, Johnson and his wife, Lady Bird, donated 201.3 acres of the ranch, including the Texas White House and outer buildings, to the National Park Service. The ranch is now part of the Johnson State Historic Park.

In 1970, both the boyhood home and birthplace house of President Johnson were given by deed to the Johnson National Historic Site, under the administration of the National Park Service. In 1980, these areas became part of the Lyndon B. Johnson National Historic Park, managed in cooperation with the adjoining Lyndon B. Johnson State Historic Park. (Courtesy National Park Service.) ▶

THE LYNDON BAINES JOHNSON LIBRARY AND MUSEUM

2313 Red River Street • Austin, Texas 78705
Tel: (512) 482-5279

Located on the University of Texas campus in Austin, one block west of I-35. Open daily from 9 A.M. to 5 P.M. Closed Christmas. No admission fee. Administered by the National Archives and Records Administration.

The library, situated on a 30-acre site, houses 35 million historical documents including the primary papers of Johnson's political career and provides year-round public viewing of historical and cultural exhibits. The eight-story building, designed by architect Gordon Bunshaft, is located across from the Lyndon Baines Johnson School of Public Affairs. It was dedicated on 22 May 1971.

▲ *More than 450,000 people visit the Lyndon Baines Johnson Library and Museum each year. The museum mounts at least two major history exhibitions per year.* (Courtesy The Lyndon Baines Johnson Library and Museum.)

FRANKLIN D. ROOSEVELT

John Devaney's *Franklin Delano Roosevelt, President* (Walker, 1987) is an excellent portrait of the only person elected four times to the presidency. It presents the person as well as the politician and describes how he dealt with adversity. (For junior high school.)

Rebecca Larsen's *Franklin D. Roosevelt: Man of Destiny* (Watts, 1991) is a well-balanced introductory biography. *Franklin Delano Roosevelt* by Russell Freedman (Clarion Books, 1990) concentrates on his political career, especially his terms as governor of New York and as president. (For junior and senior high school.)

The Age of Roosevelt, three volumes by Arthur M. Schlesinger, Jr. (Houghton Mifflin, 1965) is an excellent analysis of the life and times of the country during Roosevelt's presidency. *FDR's Splendid Deception* by Hugh G. Gallagher (Dodd, Mead, 1985) tells the story of how he coped with polio and continued his life. He went to great lengths to conceal the severity of the paralysis from the public, with the cooperation of the news media. Joseph Alsop's *FDR 1882-1945: A Centenary Remembrance* (Viking Press, 1982) is an excellent pictorial history of Roosevelt; the accompanying narrative is well done and flows well with the photos. *Roosevelt and Churchill: Their Secret Wartime Correspondence,* edited by Francis L. Loewenheim (Barrie & Jenkins, 1975), is a unique record of public policy as it was framed and implemented. It provides an enlightening description of the conduct of the war at the highest levels. The most comprehensive biography is *Franklin D. Roosevelt* by Frank B. Freidel (Little, Brown, 1952–1991), a multivolume work. (For high school and adult.)

Sharon Whitney's *Eleanor Roosevelt* (Watts, 1982) is an excellent introductory biography of the First Lady, who was the equal of her husband in many respects. (For junior high school.)

Lois Scharf's *Eleanor Roosevelt* (Twayne, 1987) is a well-researched and well-written biography. It concentrates on her development into a significant political leader in her own right. (For junior and senior high school.)

Another excellent and enjoyable book is *Eleanor Roosevelt* by Russell Freedman (Clarion Books, 1993). (For high school.)

Joseph P. Lash's *Eleanor and Franklin* (Norton, 1971) is an excellent joint biography covering the Roosevelts' personal and political lives. Lash's *Eleanor: The Years Alone* (Norton, 1972) continues her story after FDR's death, describing her life and her accomplishments during her later years. *No Ordinary Time* by Doris K. Goodwin (Simon & Schuster, 1994) is a compelling chronicle of the United States at war. It describes the Roosevelts during the war and offers a moving depiction of how ordinary Americans coped. Peter Collier's *The Roosevelt's: An American Saga* (Simon & Schuster, 1994) is an enjoyable collective biography of both branches of the Roosevelt family. It is especially good on how the personal philosophies of Theodore and Franklin developed and matured. (For high school and adult.)

There are at least two videocassette biographies of Roosevelt: *FDR: Years of Crisis* and *FDR: The War Years,* both by A&E Home Video. (For all ages.)

HARRY S. TRUMAN

Karin C. Farley's *Harry S. Truman: The Man From Independence* (Julian Messner, 1989) is a balanced introductory biography, providing information on his personal life as well as his political life. (For junior high school.)

Thomas Fleming's *Harry S Truman, President* (Walker, 1993) is an excellent description of his presidency and of the decisions he made. *Harry S. Truman* by Barbara S. Feinberg (Watts, 1994) discusses how he coped with the presidency as World War II ended and the cold war began. *President Truman and the Atomic Bomb* by Michael O'Neal (Greenhaven Press, 1990), although not a true biography, presents an excellent analysis of the events leading up to and after the dropping of the atomic bomb on Japan. It also includes some opposing viewpoints from world leaders. (For junior and senior high school.)

David McCullough's *Truman* (Simon & Schuster, 1992) is a very readable general biography of both his personal and his political lives. Robert H. Ferrell's *Harry S. Truman: A Life* (University of Missouri Press, 1994) offers new perspectives on many of Truman's foreign policy initiatives, such as the Truman Doctrine and the Marshall Plan. *Plain Speaking* by Merle Miller (G. P. Putnam's Sons, 1974) is based on hundreds of hours of conversations with Truman and offers insight and reflection on both his personal and his political lives. For a wonderful and warm biography see Margaret Truman's *Harry S. Truman* (Morrow, 1984), which deals primarily with his personal life before the presidency. Another book by Robert H. Ferrell is *Off the Record: The Private Papers of Harry S. Truman* (Harper & Row, 1980), which offers a frank assessment of Truman's presidency and his later life and is based on his diaries and papers from 1945 to 1971. *Bess W. Truman* by Margaret Truman (Macmillan, 1986) is a well-drawn portrait of Bess Truman and her remarkable marriage and political partnership. See *Dear Bess: The Letters From Harry to Bess Truman,* edited by Robert H. Ferrell (Norton, 1983), for a view from the other side of the relationship. (For high school and adult.)

DWIGHT D. EISENHOWER

Stephen E. Ambrose's *Ike/Abilene to Berlin* (Harper & Row, 1973) is a fine biography covering the years from his early boyhood to the Allied victory in Europe. Jean Darby's *Dwight D. Eisenhower* (Lerner, 1989) is a good general source for his personal, military, and political lives. *Dwight David Eisenhower: War Hero and President* by Marian G. Cannon (Watts, 1990) concentrates on his military career, especially during World War II; a short discussion of the presidency is also included. Peter Sandberg's *Dwight D. Eisenhower* (Chelsea House, 1986) is a well-done biography that emphasized his military career. (For junior and senior high school.)

The definitive biography is Stephen E. Ambrose's two volume-work *Eisenhower: Soldier, General of the Army, President-Elect, 1890-1952* (Simon & Schuster, 1983) and *Eisenhower: The President* (Simon & Schuster, 1984). Ambrose revised and consolidated these works into one volume, *Eisenhower: Soldier and President* (Simon & Schuster, 1990); both biographies are full, rich, and objective portraits of Eisenhower. *Ike: His Life and Times* by Piers Brendon (Harper & Row, 1986) is a well-researched critical examination of Eisenhower, with emphasis on his military career and the presidency. Michael R. Beschloss's *Eisenhower: A Centennial Life* (HarperCollins Publishers, 1990) is an excellent pictorial biography covering all aspects of his life. The narrative ties the photos together extremely well. *Ike, 1890–1990: A Pictorial History* by Douglas Kinnard is also a comprehensive photographic biography. *Ike and Mamie* by Lester David (G. P. Putnam's Sons, 1981) is a well-written joint biography that provides insight into their marriage. (For high school and adult.)

JOHN F. KENNEDY

Catherine C. Anderson's *John F. Kennedy, Young People's President* (Lerner, 1991) is a good introductory biography. (For junior high school.)

John F. Kennedy by Judie Mills (Watts, 1988) is a thorough and well-balanced accounting of his youth, early political career, and presidency. *John F. Kennedy* by Marta Randall (Chelsea House, 1987) is a well-illustrated chronology of the major issues in his presidency. Robert J. Donovan's *PT–109* (McGraw-Hill, 1961) recounts his wartime naval service in the Pacific. (For junior and senior high school.)

William Manchester's *One Brief Shining Moment* (Little, Brown, 1983) is a wonderful photographic history of Kennedy and the presidency. The narrative complements the photos well. *JFK: Reckless Youth* by Nigel Hamilton (Random House, 1992), the first volume of a planned multivolume biography, is based on much new unpublished material. It covers JFK's life through his election to Congress. *A Thousand Days* by Arthur M. Schlesinger, Jr. (Houghton Mifflin, 1965) is an insider's account of the events leading to Kennedy's nomination for the presidency and his subsequent election. It is also a careful analysis of his administration. Another excellent book on the Kennedy presidency is William R. Manchester's *Portrait of a President* (Little, Brown, 1967). Manchester is also the author of *The Death of a President* (Harper & Row, 1967), a long, detailed account of the days and events surrounding Kennedy's assassination. The latest book to attempt to discredit the official interpretation of the assassination is *Killing Kennedy: And the Hoax of the Century* by Harrison E. Livingstone (Carroll & Graf, 1995). Peter Collier's *The Kennedys: An American Drama* (Summit Books, 1984) is a family history of Joseph and Rose Kennedy and their children. Mark Shaw's *The John F. Kennedys* (Farrar, Straus, 1964) is a coffee-table family photo album. *My Life With Jacqueline Kennedy* by Mary B. Gallagher (David McKay, 1969) offers an intimate portrait of Jackie Kennedy as seen by the woman who was her personal secretary for eight years. (For high school and adult.)

There are at least two titles on Kennedy available on videocassette: *John F. Kennedy,* a three-cassette series by AIMS Media, and *The Assassination of JFK* by MPI. (For all ages.)

LYNDON B. JOHNSON

John Devaney's *Lyndon Baines Johnson, President* (Walker, 1986) is a very good introductory biography, highlighting his political accomplishments. Dennis Eskow's *Lyndon Baines Johnson* (Watts, 1993) captures the many facets of Johnson. *The President from Texas* by Dudley Lynch (Crowell, 1975) is a well-balanced biography of a master politician. *Lyndon B. Johnson* by Tony Kaye (Chelsea House, 1987) highlights his successes, especially the passage of civil rights legislation and of Medicare, and the devastating Vietnam War. (For junior and senior high school.)

Big Daddy from the Pedernales: Lyndon B. Johnson (Twayne, 1986) is a well-balanced treatment of his personal life and his political career. Merle Miller's *Lyndon: An Oral Biography* (G. P. Putnam's Sons, 1980) is based on interviews of people who knew him. *The Triumph and Tragedy of Lyndon Johnson* by Joseph A. Califano Jr. (Simon & Schuster, 1991) is an excellent analysis of the events of his presidency. *The Politician* by Ronnie Dugger (Norton, 1982) analyzes the man and his actions as well as the times surrounding them. Lewis L. Gould's *Lady Bird Johnson and the Environment* (University Press of Kansas, 1988) is not a true biography, but it summarizes Mrs. Johnson's Beautification of America work and discusses her impact on legislation. (For high school and adult.)

PBS Video has a two-part video set entitled *LBJ*. (For all ages.)

at a glance . . .

President	Volume	President	Volume	President	Volume
George Washington	1	James Buchanan	3	Calvin Coolidge	5
John Adams	1	Abraham Lincoln	3	Herbert Hoover	5
Thomas Jefferson	1	Andrew Johnson	3	Franklin D. Roosevelt	6
James Madison	1	Ulysses S. Grant	3	Harry S. Truman	6
James Monroe	1	Rutherford B. Hayes	4	Dwight D. Eisenhower	6
John Quincy Adams	2	James A. Garfield	4	John F. Kennedy	6
Andrew Jackson	2	Chester A. Arthur	4	Lyndon B. Johnson	6
Martin Van Buren	2	Grover Cleveland	4	Richard M. Nixon	7
William Henry Harrison	2	Benjamin Harrison	4	Gerald R. Ford	7
John Tyler	2	William McKinley	4	Jimmy Carter	7
James K. Polk	2	Theodore Roosevelt	5	Ronald Reagan	7
Zachary Taylor	3	William Howard Taft	5	George Bush	7
Millard Fillmore	3	Woodrow Wilson	5	Bill Clinton	7
Franklin Pierce	3	Warren G. Harding	5		